WALTER STEPHEN is a former Chairman o
Memorial Trust. Arthur Geddes, Patrick Gec
vised his university dissertation. Influenced t
up and ran for 20 years the first successful
Britain, in Cannonball House, apex of a triang.c whose other corners
are the Outlook Tower and Ramsay Garden. Castlehill Urban Studies
Centre was closed to make way for the Press Office for the new
Scottish Parliament.

AUBREY MANNING is Emeritus Professor of Natural History, University
of Edinburgh, with a long career specialising in the study of animal
behaviour. He was influential in making natural history accessible by
setting up 'twinning' arrangements between undergraduates and
teachers and pupils in local schools. Over the last decade he has
proved a popular and authoritative presenter of TV and radio series
such as *Earth Story, Talking Landscapes, Landscape Mysteries* and
The Sounds of Life.

JAMES MACKINNON is Chief Planner of the Scottish Executive.

MIKE SMALL is the editor of the online *Journal of Civics and Generalism*
(www.patrickgeddes.co.uk) and has been researching, publishing, writing and lecturing on Patrick Geddes since 1995. His interests lie in
applying Geddes's ideas through bioregionalism, communalism and
direct action.

KENNY MUNRO is a freelance arts consultant and sculptor, happy to be
known as a visual thinker and 'creative irritant'. His activities are
diverse; working with schools, examining phosphorescent marine
plankton and currently exploring international relationships between
river communities in Scotland, Australia and India. Once chairman of
Edinburgh Sculpture Workshop he promotes the role of the arts at the
centre of every community as an empowering tool, stimulating practical cross curricular education.

His sculptural homage to Sir Patrick Geddes, a granite and bronze
pillar entitled 'Evergreen', can be viewed at Rodney Garden, on the
river walkway in Perth.

FRANK SPAVEN studied geography with Arthur Geddes and was one of the original Patrick Geddes Trustees. As a civil servant at the Scottish Office and the first head of planning at the Highlands and Islands Development Board he was influential in public transport matters. Unsuccessful in the 'McPuff' campaign to keep the Strathmore line open, his critique of the Beeching proposals of 1963 was devastating. He was instrumental in saving the bulk of the Highland rail network from closure. To the end he was active in promoting the living legacy of Sir Patrick Geddes.

ANNE-MICHELLE SLATER is a lecturer at the School of Law, University of Aberdeen. She is interested in Geddes, as his views, exploits and endeavours regularly appear in seemingly unrelated areas of her life: a perfect example of which is the marine station at Cowie. She believes in learning by doing and gets students out of the classroom whenever possible, something of which she hopes Geddes would have approved.

SOFIA LEONARD is a Trustee of the Sir Patrick Geddes Memorial Trust. For ten years she was Director of the Patrick Geddes Centre for Planning Studies in the Outlook Tower and has an unrivalled knowledge of Geddes's works. She has travelled extensively investigating the legacy of Patrick Geddes.

A Vigorous Institution

The Living Legacy of Patrick Geddes

Introduced and edited by Walter Stephen

Contributions by
Aubrey Manning, James Mackinnon, Mike Small,
Kenny Munro, Frank Spaven, Anne-Michelle Slater
and Sofia Leonard

Luath Press Limited
EDINBURGH
www.luath.co.uk

First published 2007

All royalties generated from sales of this book will be paid to the
Sir Patrick Geddes Memorial Trust.

The paper used in this book is acid-free, neutral-sized and recyclable. It is
made from low-chlorine pulps produced in a low energy, low emission
manner from renewable forests.

Printed and bound by
Bell & Bain Ltd., Glasgow

Typeset in 10.5 point Sabon by
3btype.com

Contents

Illustrations – Colour Plates

PLATE 1
The Geddes Panels

PLATE 2A
Helen Williamson, Senior Library Officer, Department of
  Art and Music, Edinburgh Central Library, examines the
  Geddes model

PLATE 2B
Sonar Tari – Golden Boat, Kolkata, April 2004

PLATE 3A
Sonar Tari – Bengal Boat, Ballater, October 2004

PLATE 3B
Dunglass Dean – four fine bridges

PLATE 4A
Royal Border Bridge, 1964

PLATE 4B
Penmanshiel, 8 March 1979

PLATE 5A
Was Peter/Patrick Geddes born here?

PLATE 5B
Mount Tabor Cottage, Perth

PLATE 6A
Former course of Cowie Water

PLATE 6B
Stonehaven and the site of the marine station from the south

Illustrations – Figures

Acknowledgements

THE FIRST ACKNOWLEDGEMENT must be to the contributors, who have taken time out from busy lives to share with others their thoughts on Geddes and his place in the new, 21st, century. Those who remember the film *Ben-Hur* will know how difficult it was to drive a chariot with two or three horses in a busy Colosseum. As Editor I can truthfully state that a common interest in Geddes and his living legacy made the handling of these contributors an enjoyable experience.

Individuals have indicated their own sources of support. In addition, the great national institutions have been very helpful, with particular members of staff going beyond the call of duty.

The illustrations in the text referred to as FIGS 12, 13, 14 and 15 and FIG 9 have been used by courtesy of (respectively) Edinburgh University Library and Aberdeen University Library. Their kindness is hereby acknowledged. The map extracts (FIGS 7 and 8) are reproduced by kind permission of the National Library of Scotland.

Documentary evidence from the National Library of Scotland and the National Archives of Scotland (Register House and New Register House) is gratefully acknowledged. For Alexander Geddes's service record the National Archives (Army Records, Public Records Office) are thanked accordingly.

A grant from the Heritage Lottery Fund (Awards For All) made possible the publication of *A Vigorous Institution*. The Sir Patrick Geddes Memorial Trust gratefully acknowledges this support.

Walter Stephen
Editor

Introduction

Walter Stephen

Lewis Mumford published the first 'Talk from My Outlook Tower' ('A Schoolboy's Bag and A City's Pageant') by Patrick Geddes on 1 February 1925, in volume 53 of *Survey*. In the Foreword, entitled: 'Who is Patrick Geddes?' Mumford answers his own question, supposing:

> If one dropped in on a luncheon group at the faculty club of a metropolitan university and asked a dozen scholars: 'Who is Patrick Geddes?' there would probably be a dozen answers, and though some of the answers would be hazy, they would all, I think, be different; and one might get the impression that Professor Geddes is a vigorous institution, rather than a man.

This collection of essays takes the concept of a vigorous institution and re-examines Geddes's fitness so to be described. Some writers reinforce what is already generally known. Others touch on new aspects of his life and work. All, to some degree, deal with influences on Geddes and his influences on subsequent thought and action.

Saturday 2 October 2004 was a great day for anyone remotely interested in Geddes or the environment. On that date 150 years before, Geddes had been born in Ballater. It was clear that in many towns, in many countries, this anniversary was not to pass unnoticed. While some of the Sir Patrick Memorial Trust trustees were involved in events as far apart as Ballater and Japan, it was felt that, for Geddes, Edinburgh was the place which influenced him most, where his influence was greatest, and therefore the Edinburgh-based Trust should be pulling out all the stops to make the great man accessible to the public.

The anniversary excitement started late on the Friday afternoon. Earlier in the summer a small team of Geddesians had engaged to write a readable and up-to-date text for the anniversary. Despite one of the team losing time through having to undergo a surgical procedure, the phone call came through from the printer in Livingston at 4 pm –

'We've got the first of your books here now. Where do you want them delivered?' At 5.30 pm, in the Royal Museum of Scotland, Jonathon Porritt, Chair of the UK Sustainable Development Commission, reporting directly to the Prime Minister, started the First Annual Sir Patrick Geddes Commemorative Lecture, organised by the Royal Town Planning Institute in Scotland and the Saltire Society. To add to the importance and scope of the occasion, video link technology made possible the contribution and participation of the Ballater Geddes Group 2004, comfortably ensconced in the Craigendarroch Hotel, Ballater. Back in the RMS, while proposing the vote of thanks, the chairman was able to present the very first signed copy of *Think Global, Act Local: The Life and Legacy of Patrick Geddes* to Jonathon Porritt, with the commendation that it had been skimmed through and found to be very good!

From 16 September till 22 October, in the Matthew Architecture Gallery, University of Edinburgh there ran an exhibition – 'Patrick Geddes: The Regeneration of Edinburgh'. The basis of the exhibition was a framed selection of material from Geddes's papers not usually accessible to the general public. Originally prepared for the Outlook Tower and the Cities Exhibition the Geddes Collection is now kept in the Special Collections of Edinburgh University. The exhibition was an excellent example of cooperation between the Department of Architecture of the University of Edinburgh, who kindly and appropriately hosted the exhibition, and the Anniversary Symposium, the University Library, the Patrick Geddes Trust and Awards for All Scotland – who grant-aided both of these activities.

As a teacher, Geddes made full use of every medium available to him. The trust tried to do the same. We now had a room full of two-dimensional treasures – maps, diagrams, photographs, sketches – it was up to us to show how Geddes used other media. The Trust owns three stained glass panels commissioned by Geddes, which were brought together and displayed on a specially-constructed frame. The conceptual model was a favourite tool of Geddes. When he became temporarily blind in Mexico he was thrown back on to his own resources and began to link abstract reflection with simple diagrams. Some of them he called 'thinking machines'. For the Paris World's Fair of 1900 he had a decorative 'Valley Section' and *'Flos Herbae'* created – both full of symbolism. The Valley Section in particular was worked and reworked over the years to stimulate the analysis of the 'Work, Place, Folk' triad. The Outlook Tower ('the world's first sociological laboratory') used these and other resources as part of the teaching material. Murdo Macdonald, in *Think Global, Act Local,* made a deeply stimulating analysis of the 'Valley Section' which has appeared and re-appeared in many contexts since PG first used it (PLATE 1).

'Lilies' was created for Riddle's Court, the first self-governing student residence in Europe. For a century the good burghers of Edinburgh in search of education passed through the door in which it was set, perhaps noting Geddes's three doves of sympathy, synthesis and synergy. Did they know what Geddes had said about the lily?

> 'Pure as a lily' is not really a phrase of hackneyed sham-morals; for it does not mean weak, bloodless, sexless, like your moral philosopher's books, your curate's sermons. The lily's Purity lies in that it has something to be pure; its Glory is in being the most frank and open manifestation of sex in all the organic world.

Again, as a teaching tool, for the Cities Exhibition of 1910 Geddes had a copy cast of an 1829 model of Edinburgh. This shows the city at a crucial point in its development, just as the growth of the New Town had run out of steam, with the council corrupt and on the verge of bankruptcy. Predating the coming of the railway it illustrates beautifully the stagnation of Edinburgh before rapid growth was resumed mid-century. The Trust had a new master of the 1910 copy made, from which further copies could be made (PLATE 2A).

Professor Aubrey Manning officially opened the exhibition with a characteristically original and enthusiastic contribution which reminded us of Geddes the human ecologist and experimental scientist, the solid foundation on which he was to build his subtle and imaginative approach to social issues, to architecture, to town- and people-planning, the educational initiatives, his exploration of beauty in so many forms.

'Ideas In Evolution' was the title of the Anniversary Symposium. In my introduction I used a rather daring metaphor. *Gymnopédie No 1,* by Erik Satie (1866–1925), became free from copyright in 1975. Many commercial arrangements were published and it became popular with

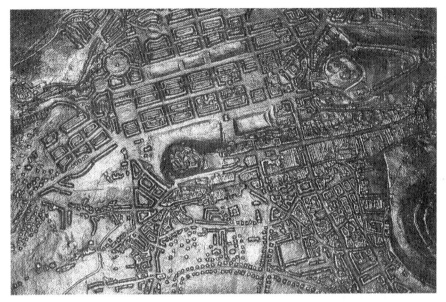

FIG I

Model of central Edinburgh (2004 replica of 1910 replica of 1824 original)
(Note: in north west, abrupt termination of New Town near Stockbridge;
in north-east, the 'New Town that never was'; also The Mound with
one art gallery and no railway.)

the more intellectual hippies. 'Lent et douloureux', it winds its slow way along in eight- and nine-bar smooth phrases each of which the poor clarinet player must sustain in a single breath. What this calm, reflective piece is meant to convey to us is a naked Greek statue seen from three different angles. Our symposium, I suggested, was like that. Geddes was in the middle, on a plinth which was rotating very slowly. Lights shone on the statue so that it appeared to change as it rotated. The speakers and events of the day would illuminate the great man, get into dark places and reflect back to our greater enlightenment.

Looking into the eyes of those assembled, I suspected there was some amused scepticism and even contempt for this notion. It was therefore with great satisfaction that I picked up, a few weeks later, *Dramatisations of History* by Patrick Geddes (Sociological Publications Ltd, London; Patrick Geddes and Colleagues, Edinburgh, 1923) and noticed the cover.

There is Geddes, naked and bearded, lying at ease over the claws of the Sphinx, in his left hand a learned scroll. His right hand helps him concentrate – or shades his eyes from the desert sun – or the intrusive lights. So I return to my metaphor and say that I see this book as a series of lights shining on Geddes. Some reveal what we already know. Some shine into dark corners to reveal something hitherto unknown. Some reflect back on to us and change our perceptions of ourselves.

Inevitably, not all that is revealed is startling. Michael Storm, in the *Bulletin of Environmental Education* (1971), attacked the looseness of some Environmental Studies at that time, thus:

FIG 2

Dramatisations of History
by Patrick Geddes – cover

Too many local studies amount to little more than the amassing of fortuitous, unrelated and unimportant facts in a parochial ragbag; how Charlie the goose was a familiar sight on the village green until killed by a car in 1967...

Is there a danger that Charlie the goose will be found stalking the pages that follow? I think not, but one must recognise that Geddes was an untidy and unsettling character who did not fit neatly into society's boxes and who was always ready to move off to the next project before the latest was completed.

We were fortunate in having as our first speaker James Mackinnon, Chief Planner, Scottish Executive. Unique among the contributors to *A Vigorous Institution* in that he has a responsibility to proffer advice and to bring about action which will still be evident in the Scottish landscape fifty years hence, his punchy and lively approach was eminently practical. His 'Lessons from Geddes' were not blind hero-worship but a clear-sighted analysis of the living legacy and the good that could be brought into the new, post-devolution Scotland through an understanding of Geddes's thought and example.

Many of those attending the symposium were the guests at a Civic Reception in the City Chambers, given by the Lord Provost and Council of the City of Edinburgh. Five Geddes grandchildren, the Trustees of the Sir Patrick Geddes Memorial Trust, the speakers, group leaders and distinguished guests attended as the City formally recognised its debt to Patrick Geddes and the Trust formed from the residue of his estate. This was no token gesture but an event of great symbolic significance.

Relationships between Geddes and the then Edinburgh establishment were, at best, edgy. The good, sensible folk of the city must have had great difficulty coping with this mercurial and disturbing character; while he often found them slow and wilfully stupid. Yet no one who could write:

> Our Edinburgh legal idea of business which eliminates all consideration of feeling, individual or public, which attains the ideal and utmost coldness to all, coinciding with the lowest circle of the Inferno – that of Ice; for your own sake and that of others, why stay there?

could expect to be loved by those same businessmen.

Odhams Press published *The Pageant of the Century* the year I was born, and it proved a constant companion on wet days for many years. A quick trawl through my battered copy gave the following:

4/4/1900	Attempt on the life of the Prince of Wales in Brussels.
29/7/1900	King Humbert of Italy fatally shot by an anarchist at Monza.
6/2/1902	M. Kantcheff, Bulgarian minister assassinated.
11/6/1903	King and Queen of Serbia murdered.
28/7/1904	Russian Minister of the Interior assassinated at St Petersburg.

1905	Attempted assassination of the Tsar. A Russian Grand Duke, the Prefect of Moscow and the Russian ex-Minister of War assassinated. Bomb thrown at the Sultan of Turkey in Constantinople; two attempts on the life of the King of Spain in Paris. Greek Prime Minister assassinated on his way to the Chamber. 160 persons injured in bomb explosion in Barcelona.
31/5/1906	Alfonso XIII and Princess Ena of Battenberg attacked by Mateo Morral, an anarchist, on their wedding day. Both unhurt, but bride spattered with blood of dead and injured spectators.
25/8/1906	Attempt on Russian Premier.
3/1/1907	Prefect of St Petersburg assassinated at Institute of Experimental Medicine.
1/2/1908	King and Crown Prince of Portugal assassinated.
23/1/1909	Outrage by aliens at Tottenham. Two Russian anarchists seizing £80 from a clerk fired indiscriminately at pursuing police and civilians.

And so on, until:

12/11/1912	Senor Canalejas, Spanish Premier, assassinated.
23/12/1912	Bomb thrown into the howdah of the elephant on which Lord and Lady Hardinge rode into Delhi to the Durbar.
18/3/1913	King of Greece shot dead.
11/6/1914	Bomb explodes in Westminster Abbey. Coronation Chair damaged.
28/6/1914	Assassination of Archduke Franz Ferdinand and his wife at Sarajevo.
31/7/1914	M. Jaures, socialist, shot dead by a young man in Paris.

Was Geddes this kind of anarchist? Geddes tried to dissociate himself from 'mere fits of despairing hysterics and threats of dynamite' – but who were in the 'Geddes group'? Prince Kropotkin was an advocate of self-help cooperation who heard of Geddes's early efforts in James Court before he met him in 1886. On release from the French prison of Clairvaux, Kropotkin made his way to James Court, where they found much to agree upon. In 1917 Geddes was to say in a letter:

> I can but express my delight over the Russian Revolution. How glad I am old Kropotkin has lived to see this!

Murdo Macdonald in *Think Global, Act Local,* reminded us that Geddes himself saw Thomas Chalmers as an anarchist economist and the Free Kirk he helped found, a reaction to government compulsion.

Perhaps understandably, the Edinburgh establishment was uneasy about the presence of anarchists at the Outlook Tower. Complaints were voiced about PG's positive use of the word 'anarchy'. He stoutly rebutted the implied criticism, that he was an anarchist, and at the same time he made clear that he had no intention of fully allying himself with anarchy, any more than with any other political philosophy. He did, however, assert that he firmly believed in the desirability of the political state to which anarchy refers, namely that it 'simply means what it says an-archy – without government i.e. without governmental compulsion'.

Ramsay Garden, Geddes's creation, is finished off with a sandstone sundial, a sermon in stone with a date (1892), a mysterious Greek inscription and a quotation from Burns. Any thoughtful citizen who made his way up to the Castle Esplanade would realise that 'It's comin' yet for a' that' is the prelude to a revolutionary aspiration:

> That Man to Man the warld o'er
> Shall brithers be for a' that.

And there were protagonists of strange faiths to be noted around the Outlook Tower and at the Summer Schools. But the Civic Reception formally recognised the great debt the City of Edinburgh now owes to Geddes, his deeds and ideas, accepting that the search for truth often creates strange bedfellows.

While we in Edinburgh were celebrating the birth of Geddes, in Yamaguchi, in south Japan, commemoration was a convenient excuse for a major Geddes-centred conference. Mike Small has taken the Japan conference and worked it into a wider consideration of Geddes's universalism, of the influences on him and of his influence on others – particularly in Cyprus, Italy, Catalonia and Japan. Most of us are familiar with what we might call 'time-line Geddes', but Mike Small analyses a Geddes influential with many contemporary innovators – a living legacy indeed.

With James Mackinnon, Mike Small is concerned about Place and from a later generation and a less traditional standpoint he anticipates the anxiety about Place central to the late Frank Spaven's paper.

The Patrick Geddes Trust deed sets out the obligation of the Trust to promote:

> the study of living society in its environment and the principles
> of regional survey, Town and Country Planning, environmental
> conservation, and the preservation of open spaces.

Geddes liked triads and believed in Dewey's education of Head, Heart and Hand. For Geddes the making of a box was a whole curriculum. In the latter half of the 20th century the structure of a desirable education system was intellectualised into the domain of the cognitive, the affective and the psycho-motor, all of which were necessary for a complete individual. Insight into the affective domain is provided by Kenny Munro, who examines the influence of Patrick Geddes on practising artists and community activities. As a member of the Ballater Geddes Group – who have chosen an environmental/aesthetic approach in relation to the local community – he shows how he was influenced by Geddes and how, in turn, he has worked at home and abroad in interpreting Geddes's ideas today, ensuring that they are a living legacy. He gives us examples of where he and others have been able to 'Act Local' and thereby encourage people to 'Think Global'.

Passing through Inverness as a teenager, I picked up a pamphlet called *The Highlands and Islands: A Regional Survey*, by two people called Arthur Geddes and Frank Spaven. Those were great days in the Highlands. New hydro-electric schemes were bringing 'power to the glens'; the Forestry Commission was reducing our dependence on foreign supplies by planting up the man-made deserts of the hills. Lord Lovat near Beauly and a Canadian distiller in the Great Glen were showing the way in the rearing of cattle on a large scale, while Frank Fraser Darling, through his *West Highland Survey*, his books and his example, seemed to be showing a new future for crofting. A few years later the establishment of a great new aluminium smelter at Invergordon and a balancing pulp and paper mill at the other end of the Great Glen seemed almost to complete the transformation of the Highlands into a Scandinavian-type region. In this atmosphere the Geddes/Spaven book was, quite simply, inspiring.

When I told Frank Spaven this, many years later, he protested, with characteristic modesty, 'But I only did the maps'. But it was the maps that I had found most exciting and inspiring! Much later I joined him on the Sir Patrick Geddes Memorial Trust, of which he was a founder member. His particular interest was in getting young people involved, not in the blind worship of Geddes and his works, but in the consideration of issues that would have concerned Geddes had he been alive in our time. The Trust has had Geddes Student Prizes of different kinds over the years and in 2000 Frank wrote a paper which was intended for advance circulation to students, who would then be asked to react to it.

FIG 3

Patrick Geddes Trust Awards Scheme – poster for students

This did not happen. What started as a page 'On Not Losing Place' became 'Overkill', more substantial and more fundamental – but still with the insistence on the restitution of the Work, Place, Folk triad. For a few weeks after the Twin Towers disaster, perhaps naively, we thought that there might be a positive outcome, that the great powers might now begin to lead the world in eliminating state-sponsored terrorism in Israel and Ireland and in moving towards sustainable living.

This comes through in 'Overkill', which is interesting because it represents the distillation of over half a century's contemplation and experience. Some may find his conclusion too simple and unrealistic, like proposing to attack an armoured giant with a scrap of leather and a few rounded pebbles from the burn. But Frank was a serious optimist; serious, yes, but an optimist always.

Interesting, too, to note, early in 2007, how quickly public opinion can swing from indifference to concern for the future and a wish to make a difference.

If evidence were needed that Frank had a lifelong interest in railways one need only look at FIG 5 – Innerwick signal box in 1931. Then realise that his paper that follows was probably the last thing he wrote. His obituaries record his role in the (unsuccessful) 'MacPuff' campaign to keep the Strathmore Line open and his influence – successful – in ensuring that Thurso, Wick and Kyle still have a rail connection. Geddes must have travelled the East Coast Main Line hundreds of times and experienced the thrill of coming back over the Royal Border Bridge to Edinburgh and Scotland.

I see Frank's paper as a later parallel to Angus Graham's *Archaeology on a Great Post Road,* which covers – literally – the same territory for another form of transport. Geddes talked about Sympathy, Synthesis and Synergy; Frank – steeped in Geddes as he was – shows Sympathy through survey and Synthesis through his analysis. One suspects that – for the railways – Synergy (action through working together) is beyond the capacity of 21st century man – yet Frank's cool appraisal makes us wonder about the sanity of a society that throws away more than 150 years of cumulative enterprise and expertise.

When we come to my own three essays it might be said that Charlie the goose has returned to the banks of the Dee or of the Elbe. Not at all. These pieces, slight though they may be, shine into dark corners and add to our understanding of the great man – and his first wife, Anna Morton. Geddes was baptised Peter. His precise place of birth was unknown till now. Yet the details of his upbringing are well known and we must admire the strength of the home which gave him the self-confidence to 'do his own thing' and still make his way in the world.

Until Sofia Leonard publishes her definitive study of Patrick Geddes and Anna Morton, 'Miss Geddes's Dresden Establishment' leads us some way towards a realisation of the processes which helped to form the character of Anna Morton, without whom Geddes would have been lost. Geddes, Van Loon and Mumford were all giants in their time. For a brief period they came together in an enterprise which, at the very least, tells us a great deal about Geddes and his views. It is from this cooperative venture that the title of our book derives.

Mumford's metaphor – A Vigorous Institution – may be different from mine, but both convey the same message – here is a man who repays close study from many different angles.

By choosing his own career path, Geddes denied himself some of the rites of passage common to others – like graduation. Nevertheless, by 1878 Geddes had decided that his student days were over and he was now ready to take up an important biology-related post. Yet only in 1888 did he become Professor of Botany, University College, Dundee, thereby achieving a degree of professional recognition and partial financial security. In those ten years he cast around vigorously for opportunities, but there must have been times when the present was depressing and the future dark.

Anne-Michelle Slater illuminates for us an interesting and little-known enterprise at Cowie, Stonehaven, which was Geddes's first real autonomous task. It could be seen as the first step in a brilliant career in experimental science. Unfortunately, the next step, a British Association-financed field visit to Mexico, resulted in darkness for Geddes; real darkness in the shape of temporary blindness and the metaphorical darkness of self-doubt, apprehension and the knowledge that the career of experimental scientist was no longer possible.

We have already noted how Geddes the educator used every technique known at the time to inform and influence his students and the general public. A poor public speaker, his diagrams, sketches and conceptual models ('thinking machines') electrified his listeners. Like the medieval cathedral-builders he used public art and sculpture, not just to beautify, but to indoctrinate the public. The pageant, the parade, the performance, each had its significance, not just as entertainment and celebration, but as a community-builder. In the Outlook Tower he turned the Camera Obscura from a voyeuristic tourist attraction into the key trigger for a concentric study of Man in his Environment. The year before McLuhan was born, Geddes's *Cities Exhibition* left visitors dizzy with the message while the medium was untidy, even chaotic.

For the First Planning Survey of Edinburgh, Geddes had over 240 photographs taken. As the Edinburgh section of the *Cities Exhibition* (1910), the survey had an international circulation. The photographs were, of course, illustrations but the survey was innovative in that it was planned as a model of how to make a City Survey. This is an agenda for action, not a celebration of Edinburgh's beauty. So we have survey/diagnosis, but the photographs point towards synthesis/planning, with an implication of synergy/cooperative action. Sympathy, Synthesis, Synergy, the three doves seen so often in Geddes symbolism. Sofia Leonard was the driving force in rescuing, classifying and interpreting the Survey photographic plates and shares with us her understanding of the purpose and value of the photographic survey.

A Vigorous Institution? Eleven essays, varied in content and style, but with the cumulative effect of reminding us yet again of the intellectual and moral force of one of our greatest Scots, not an inert icon, but a vigorous institution still. These are tangible testaments to the force of Geddes's life and work, but more important is the living legacy; the dozens of followers who are trying to put into effect in the 21st century ideas and suppositions he was pouring forth in his own lifetime.

The Regeneration of Edinburgh by Patrick Geddes

Aubrey Manning

I HAVE ALWAYS ENJOYED inventing imaginary conversations between people with whom one would like to have interacted. W.G. Grace and Brian Lara perhaps, John Muir and Frank Fraser Darling, but then, most certainly, Patrick Geddes and James Lovelock! Geddes would instantly recognise Lovelock's approach to life and the planet as a holistic system because he had always recognised this himself – he remains a completely modern thinker. A few threads of newly obtained wisdom from Lovelock, and Geddes would immediately understand the threats we now face.

We live at a time when we are slowly being forced to recognise that the huge advances made by the application of specialised, reductionist science and technology will not be enough to secure a future for humanity. Whilst the rich nations can surround themselves with ever increasing amounts of sophisticated gadgetry to buffer ourselves, many poorer nations still face the age old issues of survival. Now we can all recognise that our species shares a common set of problems which arise from our common home on the Earth, the way in which we use its resources and the way we interact with one another. We need to develop a new 'human ecology' which recognises both constraints and possibilities for advance. Lovelock is doing this now with all the developments around the theme of Gaia which recognise the planet's unique capacities to support life through interactions with it. Geddes would pick up on this and, of course, relate it to his own burgeoning ideas on human society, our relationship with the environment and the nature of ecologically sensitive human settlements.

Others in this assembly can better illuminate Geddes's extraordinary life. As a biologist I can easily relate to the evolution of the academic side of his early career. It is fascinating to see how, from the outset, he seemed to search for a biology which dealt with organisms in relation to their environment. He certainly didn't like the dry, laboratory-based botany with which he began study at Edinburgh and, somewhat improbably, it was with Thomas Henry Huxley in London that he found a freedom and a critical but receptive atmosphere in which he began to study independently.

Then came France, and a crucial exposure at Roscoff. Here the sandy beaches famously turn bright green at low tide as myriads of flatworms – *Convoluta roscoffensis* – whose skin is packed with green algae living within, rise to the surface to allow these single-celled plants to photosynthesise. Geddes was one of the pioneers in the study of such symbiosis – the close association of two organisms from which both derive benefit. We now know that such associations played a key role billions of years ago in the evolution of the cells which make up all complex forms of life.

However in the 1870s Geddes was describing – often for the first time – the way animals, lacking themselves the ability to synthesise complex molecules using the light energy from the sun, could by sheltering single-celled plants benefit from their chlorophyll. He wrote some papers on the distribution of chlorophyll in animals which were classics of their type. Darwin wrote to him with special congratulations.

Returning to Edinburgh, Geddes began teaching a wide range of biology and quickly demonstrated his skills as a teacher and his fervour in bringing living material into the laboratory as often as possible. He seemed destined for an academic career, was recommended for a chair in St Andrews, failed to get it but then tried for the newly vacant botany chair in Edinburgh. Geddes seems to have put a great deal of effort into this application; one feels certain he really wanted the position. He ranged internationally for referees to support him and a star-studded list they were. They included Thomas Henry Huxley, Alfred Russel Wallace, August Weismann and one whose letter is worth quoting in full:

Dear Sir,

I have read several of your biological papers with great interest, and I have formed, if you will permit me to say so, a high opinion of your abilities. I can entertain no doubt that you will continue to do excellent service in advancing our knowledge in several branches of science. Therefore I believe that you are well fitted to occupy any chair of natural history, for I am convinced that example is fully as important as precept for students.

I remain, dear Sir, yours faithfully,
Charles Darwin.

This was written early in the last year of Darwin's life and surely reflects as well as anything the high esteem in which Geddes was held amongst his peers. I emphasise this because the quite extraordinary range of his work and the influence which followed may perhaps overshadow the fact that Geddes was a fine research worker and field biologist. Nevertheless he didn't get the Edinburgh chair – and that turns out to have been good luck for all of us. Later he was appointed to the botany chair in Dundee, which involved his presence only during the summer terms. We now know he was not exactly idle during the rest of the year.

Despite the huge range of his interests, Geddes did continue to make important contributions to biology, both fundamental and for teaching, throughout his life. I think that it was his inherent 'awareness' as a biologist that served as the intellectual springboard from which his other contributions developed. He was an exponent of 'human ecology' before the term was ever applied. (I believe it first appeared in the subtitle to Frank Fraser Darling's *West Highland Survey* of 1955).

My pleasant duty today is to open the exhibition 'The Regeneration of Edinburgh by Patrick Geddes' and some of you may be wondering when I am going to get to that topic. Let me remind you that Geddes saw that humans best flourished in an environment with which they were in balance, both spiritually and physically. From this human extension of an essentially biological conception came all his subtle and imaginative approach to social issues, the architecture, the town-planning, the educational initiatives, his exploration of beauty in so many forms. Others have discussed and will continue to discuss Geddes's remarkable influence in their fields. The exhibition reminds us how fortunate we are in Edinburgh to have so many physical signs of his work and ideas around us still.

As a biologist, in opening this exhibition I want to salute Geddes as a great biologist whose holistic approach to the world and human societies in it is an early example of the kind of thinking which we must discover and develop again if we as a species are to have a long-term future.

Making Planning Respected and Respectable: Lessons from Geddes

James Mackinnon

THANK YOU FOR THE INVITATION to address this symposium, which is being held 150 years to the day that Patrick Geddes was born.

Fifty years ago Lord Holford said at the centenary of Geddes's birth – 'I am here as President for the time being of the Town Planning Institute and for the simple reason that the Institute without Geddes would hardly have existed'.

I can hardly say that without Geddes the Scottish Executive would not have existed. That would be stretching Geddes's influence too far. And I am not at all sure he would have wanted the label Grandfather or even Second Cousin to the Scottish Executive added to Father of British Town Planning.

I studied planning as a post-graduate and I found some of Geddes's teaching difficult to grasp, and even with the benefit of age (which is indisputable) and maturity (which is debateable), I still find him a complex character and difficult to assess. But it is clear that I am not alone in that. The planning historian Gordon Cherry wrote of Geddes:

> Making an intellectual contribution to town planning, he complemented and enriched the work of others. The trouble was that even among the intellectuals of his day, he was an extreme and often incomprehensible man. Perhaps he left ordinary mortals a little unsure.

This ordinary mortal remains a little unsure. So I am grateful to Walter Stephen for giving me a pretty broad remit. I certainly do not feel qualified to assess the impact of Geddes. Others, including many here today, are better able than I to do that. Indeed Helen Meller concluded that 'assessing Geddes's impact on the nascent planning movement is not at all straightforward'. Which is a lot kinder than Anthony Sutcliffe, who wrote 'that the task of developing planning theory was left to Patrick Geddes, who took it up with gusto and made a complete hash of it'.

Nor do I feel there is any point in trying to assess what Geddes might have thought of specific issues or proposals that are relevant today. That strikes me as a tad fatuous and somewhat presumptuous. I can't imagine Geddes would have been at all enamoured with someone, particularly a civil servant, waxing lyrical about what he might have thought.

So what I thought I might do is consider the challenges of planning reform and consider the extent to which these are underpinned by Geddes's teaching or indeed run counter to what he argued. I suppose my main thesis is that the bases of the reforms have the concepts of place and space at their core but they need to be seen in the context of current political structures, institutional arrangements and contemporary cultural and social attitudes.

In Geddes's lifetime planning moved from quite a narrow preoccupation with public health and housing. He did not live long enough, though, to witness the birth of the modern welfare state. There were five giants to slay:

- Poverty
- Disease
- Ignorance
- Idleness
- Squalor

Planning was seen as part of the solution to these problems.

As Bob Grieve pointed out:

It is difficult to convey the power of this focus on re-planning our society. There was an urge to renovate and reconstruct on more pleasant and equitable lines; and on the basis of more participation by the folk of the country themselves.

Not everyone agreed though. Winston Churchill opined:

All this stuff about planning and compensation and betterment. Broad vistas and all that. But give to me the 18th century alley, where foot-pads lurk, and the harlot plies her trade, and none of this new-fangled planning doctrine.

Much was expected of planning in that post-war period. Visionary plans were the order of the day. On the subject of vision, a friend, not a planner and somewhat sceptical about the profession, was asked who Geddes was. He replied that Geddes was a botanist who lost his vision, which is why he became a town planner! All too many of the post-war plans demonstrated the fine line between vision and hallucination and were never implemented. And perhaps we should be grateful for that because the legacy of post-war planning gave us the 29 comprehensive development areas in Glasgow, the Birmingham Bull Ring and Cumbernauld Town Centre. Perhaps if Geddes's 'conservative surgery' had been applied to urban renewal and urban expansion, planning might have fewer pejorative associations than it has now.

When I asked my colleagues what they thought were the successes of planning in the post-war period, they referred to the prevention of urban sprawl, clear separation of town and country, conservation of the built heritage. New towns were mentioned but in a slightly ambivalent way. But I guess what struck me was that the achievements they listed are mainly related to the regulatory side of planning. Examples of positive planning did not spring readily to mind and many are quite small scale. Indeed it is difficult to think of recent examples of positive planning which have or will result in what Sam Galbraith called the conservation areas of tomorrow. The one exception I can think of on any scale is Edinburgh Park.

The planning system today is not seen as a driver, far less central to progressive reform. Business interests in general and developers in particular feel that the system is over-bureaucratic, slow to respond to commercial and economic needs, and unpredictable in its outcomes. In other words, planning is a brake on economic growth. But the public, and community and voluntary groups see the planning system as complex, intimidating, unresponsive to environmental or social concerns and not transparent.

Key priorities for the Scottish Executive relate to economic growth, provision of public infrastructure, waste management facilities and affordable housing. Yet planning is not seen as a mechanism for delivery but an obstacle, something that cannot be avoided, a barrier that has to be overcome. Although I do feel that there is a tendency to place policy deficiencies or failures in other areas at the door of planning.

I think the late First Minister, Donald Dewar, caricatured what people think of planning – for the layman, a submerged, highly technical world surfacing occasionally in lengthy, often incomprehensible hearings seen as a triumph not for clarity but for the legal profession. That is far removed from what Geddes thought planning should be about – but as always with good caricatures it contains a fundamental truth.

The pressures to reform the planning system are significant and growing. But it is notoriously difficult to reform.

One of the key strengths of planning is its ability to embrace economic, social and environmental considerations. Chris Shepley, the former Chief Planning Inspector in England, commented recently that all planning students have been at the lecture that says that planning brings together the economic, social and environmental but we may have missed the lecture which tells us how to do that.

I recall recently watching a television programme set in the 1950s where the mother was at pains to tell her daughters that 'I want doesn't get'. But we are now in a society where 'I want' and 'I get' are pretty much synonymous for many people. Increasingly we have moved to a culture of rights rather than responsibilities.

It is not just about wanting and getting. It is about getting now. And that is a major problem for an activity that is not fundamentally concerned with now. Planning is about the future, which must of course be based on an understanding of past and present. And while I fully subscribe to the notion that planning must be flexible and responsive, when we deal with land, infrastructure and property, the scope for endless handbrake turns is limited.

Planning must respect individual rights but it does operate in the public interest. And planning decisions which are taken for the good of all of us may impact on individual rights. I can understand why people get upset about some planning decisions. No one wants a waste disposal site or quarrying operation in close proximity. But, in other cases, concerns seem to be motivated more by the impact of development on property values or a minor change in personal amenity. In a fast changing and increasingly confusing world I guess being able to hold on to familiar sights or landmarks becomes important.

And of course something that operates in the long-term public interest has to be overseen by the public sector. And I guess confidence in the public sector, and the civil service in particular, is not that high right now. There is, of course, more of what is called accountability these days, although blame may be a more accurate description. But processes and decisions are more closely scrutinised by politicians, regulatory and audit bodies and the courts. So Geddes's statement that 'I cannot and will not keep accounts' – with which I would certainly sympathise – might not play too well. With that approach, he certainly would have found himself in the firing line had he been placed in charge of the Holyrood project!

So the challenges we face in reforming the planning system are very significant, particularly as different interests are looking for different things from reform. But I believe the process of reform will have a greater chance of success if some of the fundamental principles and approaches that Geddes advocated are kept in the forefront of our consciousness.

Geddes's philosophy was rooted in place. I don't just mean bricks and mortar – it is about places in a wider and deeper sense. The term spatial planning is now very much in vogue although, to an old stager like me, I had always thought that was the purpose of planning – whether at the national, regional, local or neighbourhood level. Planning is about understanding places and guiding their future development. It is about where things should happen and where they should not. And when the decision is taken to develop, it is about how it should happen.

I believe that planners are less good at understanding places than they were. The art and science of survey are all but gone. So many of the plans I read could be about anywhere. They invariably start by doffing their caps in the direction of economic competitiveness, social justice, sustainable development, environmental protection. Would you really expect to see a policy on community safety on the first page of a structure plan for a remote rural area?

In between the aspirations and the policies there is material on housing, employment, retailing, transport, environment: but remarkably little on what makes places as they are and what they might be. We have concentrated on understanding the external forces driving change – household formation, impact of the knowledge economy, shopping preferences etc. These are important considerations but there has been a general failure, neglect, unwillingness – call it what you will – to understand the ability of places to drive or accommodate change.

We have also witnessed an emphasis on the thematic at the expense of the spatial. More and more we have looked at subjects such as housing, employment, retailing, transport, in isolation. Take housing, for example. There is an understandable imperative to provide sufficient land for housing – not in my view as part of a long term settlement strategy but, instead, as providing enough land for housing right now. I think we in the Scottish Executive have been culpable in that. Our Scottish Planning Policy series is thematic. I am not suggesting that the planning profession should not have in-depth understanding of specific issues but we need to be better able to tease out and explain what they mean for places.

Place and space must be at the absolute heart of planning education, training and practice. As Geddes observed, planning cannot be done in the office with ruler and parallels – for the plan must be sketched out on the spot, after wearying hours of perambulation. I am not sure that plans being sketched out on the spot is the answer – QCs would have fun with that at planning inquiries. But understanding a place – its physical, social, economic, cultural and environmental characteristics – is a fundamental prerequisite of good planning.

I think there are big issues here for the training of planners. My planning education was not particularly spatial. It was most certainly not rooted in place. Planners whom we have recently recruited to the Executive have told me that their courses were essentially thematic.

I think there is a big challenge for the planning schools in developing courses that enable students to come away with a sound understanding of the way places function and their prospects for change. Planners should not be general policy wonks but professionals with specific and recognisable and, I would like to think, better rewarded skills.

I think we also have to recognise that some planners have the ability and potential to perform well at the regional or indeed national level in this area while others demonstrate an aptitude for master planning and the regulation of development. We need to recognise that while both skill sets are valid, one is not of a higher order than the other. But at present I feel so much in the education system is aimed at a middle ground which does not allow the skills at different levels to develop and flourish.

The last observation is based on my dealings with planners from continental Europe and Scandinavia, where those who practise what the Germans call 'Raumplanning', literally spatial planning, have a different background and tradition from those who practise 'Städtebau' or town planning. The former are most likely to be geographers or economists, the latter architects. They are confident with that distinction and their respective contributions appear to be better understood and valued.

I believe that the Executive has made a real attempt to get to grips with issues of space and place with the production of the first ever National Planning Framework for Scotland. It is a document which looks at Scotland as a place and how it is changing. As the Permanent Secretary of the Scottish Executive commented recently, there are signs that we are gaining confidence not just to understand the future but also to shape it. The publication of the National Planning Framework marks a significant first step in that direction.

At the other end of the spectrum we have Designing Places. This did not come from an elitist approach to urban design. Quite the contrary. Terms such as defensive permeability – fences or railings to you or me – or legibility were banned. Designing Places was about demystifying urban design and raising the standards of development in urban and rural Scotland, based on the principles of:

- Identity
- Safe and pleasant places
- Ease of movement
- Sense of welcome
- Adaptability
- Good use of resources

But Geddes was right that:

town planning is not something that can be done from above, on general principles easily laid down, which can be learned in one place and imitated in another... it is the development of local life, a regional character, a civic spirit, a unique individuality, capable of course of growth and expansion... of profiting too by the example of criticism of others, yet always in its own way and upon its own foundations.

We are proposing to modernise the development plan system in Scotland. At the very heart of these reforms are city region plans which gel completely with Geddes's thinking. These plans must contain a clearly articulated long term strategy, not a list of thematic or criteria-based policies.

But we do need to get development plans in place. I am afraid that our record on local planning is poor. Over 40 per cent of local plans were adopted years ago. What confidence can investors, communities and decision makers have in plans that are so rooted in the past? Lord Gill's comment about planners in leisurely pursuit of a real world that is accelerating away from them has a worrying ring of truth about it.

We need plans that will engage individuals and communities. Plans that will command widespread support and confidence. And, of course, plans that will lead to action.

The first and last of these points are, of course, connected. If a plan is not going to make a difference, why get involved? If areas are going to experience no more than modest or incremental change, then plans should say so in so many words. Complex expositions of what is little more than the status quo undermine the relevance, accessibility and credibility of planning.

We need to engage individuals and communities more effectively in the planning process. We published research recently which showed just how skewed public involvement in planning really was. I do not underestimate the scale of the task but we need to find ways of ensuring more widespread and earlier engagement or involvement so that individuals and communities play a fuller role in shaping their places. But there has to be greater acceptance that dissatisfaction with an outcome does not mean that the process is deficient, defective or corrupt.

There needs to be a step change in the quality of the plans themselves. Even professional planners find plans difficult to understand

and interpret. They must be written in language that is easily understood. That might rule out Geddes, whom Bob Grieve thought wrote in a mannered and cumbersome style. In fact he went so far as to describe it as a kind of sub-Carlylean English. I am not quite sure what that is but it does not sound particularly complimentary.

We tend to bemoan the involvement of lawyers in planning yet I feel that so many plans are written like conveyancing documents they almost invite legal scrutiny. It is the boxing equivalent of leading with the chin. We need plans that clarify the issues, not obscure them. I find it difficult to believe that a development plan for a remote island community needs to contain 180 policies on 400 pages.

Geddes passionately believed that plans that did not lead to actions were useless. I feel that too many of today's plans are little more than policy compendia that provide a basis for controlling or regulating development. But I am sure that this function, important – indeed essential – though it is, could be done as effectively, if not more effectively, without documents that corralled everything that moved. The positive side of planning, the promotion of development, redevelopment and management of resources has not been as prominent as it should be. Technical merit and artistic impression are all very well but the plans are there to make a difference. And we have certainly taken up Geddes's dictum with our proposals for action plans updated every two years.

That seems to be a simple concept and one with which few could disagree. But it has spawned questions such as: Should these action plans be statutory? Should their content be prescribed in regulation? Should they be approved by the Scottish ministers?

This brings me back to Donald Dewar's point about planning. We have real aspirations to make planning a respected and respectable activity, not central to everything, but having a seat at the top table. Not a dragon that requires to be slain to get to the promised land, but a fellow traveller with particular skills and responsibilities. Yet there is a danger that the objectives of reform get bogged down in detail of process and procedure.

Our job at the Scottish Executive is to provide the legislative and policy framework to achieve the wider objectives of reform. And that means we have to resolve issues such as: Where should the boundaries of city region plans be drawn? Should strategic environmental assessment apply to modifications made by Scottish Ministers to structure plans? Should responsibility for neighbour notification be given to councils? Should the definition of a neighbour be changed? How much planning control should there be over mobile phone installations, etc.?

And, of course, we have to engage with the political process. Not as an optional extra, but as a constant. Geddes had a profound distrust of the political machine. Indeed, one of his biographers, much later, made the point that he had taken 'the fatal step of ignoring political debate'. I am afraid that is not an option that is open to me. Indeed, the greater involvement and exposure to the political process since devolution has been a positive and welcome development.

I could go on. But the point I want to make is that our job is to devise a planning system, with all its attendant processes, procedures, checks and balances, that is respected, not just for *what* it is seeking to achieve, but *how* it is seeking to achieve it. Geddes's philosophy, ideals and approach remain as relevant as when he taught; in fact, I would argue that we need to put place-making at the centre of our reform agenda.

I mentioned Lord Holford at the start of my address and it is a fitting way to bring my ramblings to an end with a quote from his speech at Geddes's centenary:

The Greek epigram on Plato is applicable to him – wherever I go in my mind, I meet Geddes coming back.

And if we keep the essentials of Geddes's approach and philosophy in our minds as we finalise and implement our proposals to modernise and reform the planning system, then we will make real progress in achieving our goal of making planning respected and respectable.

Universalism and the *Genus Loci:* Geddes in Cyprus, Italy, Catalonia and Japan

Mike Small

THE SIGNIFICANCE OF Patrick Geddes's impact across fields of enquiry, most notably neo-humanism, socio-ecology, localism, regionalism and cultural revival, is only beginning to be unearthed in Scotland and now, also, much further afield. This hit home as I sat with two colleagues in the Ueno Park in Tokyo in 2004. We were returning from a conference in Yamaguchi in the south of the Japan that was celebrating the 150th anniversary of Geddes's birth.

As we enjoyed the twilight of the vast city, a haunting music floated over the park announcing its imminent closure. Despite the traditional Japanese instruments used in the rendition it was, we realised un-mistakenly, 'Auld Lang Syne'. It was an appropriately astonishing ending to what had been an inspiring journey to meet students, scholars and practitioners of Geddes's ideas on the other side of the world.

This universal appeal needs exploration. We know something of Geddes's influence and experience of France, from Roscoff to Montpellier (via Paris), and biography has even touched on his travels in Mexico, India and to a lesser extent America, but we know much less of his work elsewhere. This is a rough sketch of how Geddes's ideas came to land on the far shores of Cyprus, Italy, Catalonia and even-tually Japan.

Man and Nature

This is to wilfully set aside for a moment the westward trajectory of Geddes's ideas, which, in an environmental context, are diffuse yet amazingly focused and impactful. He collides and interplays with other writers, such as Vermont's pre-figurative eco-philosopher George Perkins

Marsh (1801–1882), whose *Man and Nature* (1864) intended to show that: 'whereas others think that the earth made man, man in fact made earth'.

The message was crystal clear: if man could ruin nature maybe he could also restore it.

In an era in which global warming is the single biggest threat to mankind it is no mystery why Geddes, who wrote of 'carboniferous capitalism' should hold attention across the world. As the American writer David Lowenthal says:

After a period of relative neglect, *Man and Nature* was resurrected by those made newly aware of the perils of floods and soil erosion by Dust Bowl and other disasters of the 1930s. Through the agency of the Scottish planner Patrick Geddes, the polymath reformer Lewis Mumford 'rediscovered' the book as early as 1924.

Lowenthal concludes: 'Almost every conservation text today salutes *Man and Nature* as the beginning of land wisdom.'

But the unfolding exchanges of these pioneers of the modern environmental movement were to criss-cross the Atlantic and the Pacific. Lowenthal again writes:

Europeans put Marsh's precepts to use sooner than Americans. The French geographer Elisé Reclus owed much to Marsh for his *La Terre* (1868). Italian foresters (Siemoni, Boccardo, Di Berenger) found Marsh's work of huge value; Italy's 1877 and 1888 forest laws embody citations from Marsh, who persuaded Italians to stress restoration above mere preservation. *Man and Nature* inspired Dietrich Brandis and others stemming forest destruction in India; echoing Hayden, forest conservator Hugh Cleghorn told Marsh: 'I have carried your book with me' into the Himalayas, Kashmir, and Tibet. Before 1900, Marsh's insights inspired scholars and conservators in Australia, New Zealand, South Africa and Japan.

As the ideas of ecology, regionalism and democracy traversed the oceans, Geddes was ready to acknowledge the influence of Marsh, whom he saw as a necessary complement to Gibbon's *Decline and Fall of the Roman Empire*:

> Marsh was able to see with new clearness the far more terrible ruin of old Italy, as indeed of all Mediterranean lands through the destruction of the forests.

And, if Geddes was to frequently recount Marsh's warning that drought and famine in the Mediterranean region was the inevitable consequence of deforestation since the dawn of civilization (an issue we'll see he returned to in Cyprus), their common ground was not exclusive to environmental concerns. When Marsh writes:

> Just as someone who has mastered the ordinary use of a wide vocabulary [was often] a better speaker and even writer than the profoundest theoretical grammarian, so did diffusion of a wide range of knowledge and culture make better citizens – he could have been Geddes.

This concept of generalism has been kept aloft above the waves of specialism and professionalism for the last century, and survived through to Yamaguchi in 2004.

Geddes's ideas had further influence across the Americas through Lewis Mumford, Benton Mackay and on down into today's thwarted, delayed but 'coming yet' bioregionalist movement, via (amongst others) planner Peter Berg in San Francisco and poet Gary Snyder. In *Cities and Evolution* (1915), Geddes wrote that:

> Each place has a true personality, which it is the task of the planner, as master-artist, to awaken. And only he can do this who is in love and at home with his subject.

It is the awakening of the importance of place in the context of ecological crises that has resonance in all countries today.

But it is the journey *east* that is the subject of this short essay. In travelling east with Geddes we follow the diaspora of ideas that came and went with the Scots who ventured out. This diaspora is now being re-united and rightly revisited a century on, as two forces collide. Force One: the re-discovery of the 'local' as a potent and vital element in resisting the onslaught of empire, the anti-ecological imperative and the bland culture of mass media and pan-global (in-)corporation. Force Two: its counterweight, the global celebration of diversity, commonality and internationalism, fostered by the anti-globalisation movement. Disputes over trade (and the potential for fair and feral alternatives) are matched by the ongoing crises in food production, health and agriculture – while the state and vested interests fail to suppress the ready options that present themselves.

In this context it is no wonder that Geddes's voice seems clarion clear today, 100 years after he read 'Civics as Applied Sociology' to the first meetings of the British Sociological Society. If all of Marsh's pre-millennial eco-warnings have been proven horribly accurate, maybe that is why everywhere you travel Geddes's influence can be seen. If Marsh was to inspire Geddes and Reclus, let us start where Marsh pointed Geddes to: the Mediterranean.

Genus Loci

Let us look briefly at Geddes's influence in the area, one historical and one which has taken many years to come to fruition. The second is his efforts towards solving a crisis of Armenian refugees, with experiments in community development. In Cyprus he is little known. The first, where his ideas filtered through to Catalan revivalists, craftsmen and town planners, is little acknowledged.

Catalan *Modernismo*, a cultural and artistic style of the late 19th and early 20th centuries, was the Spanish equivalent of the Arts and Crafts movement and Art Nouveau, the German *Werkbund* and the Viennese Secession.

A whole other book could and should be committed to the connections and cooperation between the movements of Celtic Revival and Catalan *Modernismo*. Both shared a search for ideals of a new concept of beauty based on the creative essence of humankind. Through the work of the Spanish academic Juan Martinez-Alier we are seeing the lasting influence of Geddes in the environmental justice movement and in the burgeoning field of ecological economics.

But the most obvious expression of *Modernismo* is through architecture, and various practitioners – Antoni, Lluís Domènech i Montaner, Josep Puig i Cadafalch – developed personal styles that have transformed Barcelona into the city it is today.

While Gaudí's star shines so bright it excludes the vision of others, the Catalan architect Josep Puig i Cadafalch (1867–1956) was highly influential in the urban transformation of Barcelona and owes a great debt to Geddes.

As the *New Yorker* writer and 'new urbanist' Alex Marshall writes:

Barcelona has a variety of ambitious, far-reaching plans. Most revolve around making the city more hospitable to families, and keeping jobs and industries sprinkled throughout the city. In its Gothic quarter, the city has selectively blown up blocks of thousand-year old buildings to create new public squares and open up the network of tiny, dark streets to sunlight. It is a program that might set a preservationist's teeth on edge, but it is an admirable example of an effort to keep a historic section of a city livable and not just a museum. It falls within the definition of 'constructive urban surgery' advocated by the early 20th century urban theorist, Patrick Geddes. In the *Eixample*, the city has begun converting the interior of some blocks to neighborhood parks, which essentially was the original plan of architect Ildefons Cerda i Sunyer, who laid out the *Eixample* in 1859. In older industrial areas of the city, close to the Olympic village, the city plans to extend streets to reshape street systems back to Cerda's original soft-cornered grid. All these plans are ambitious and purely urban in their vision.

The curve as core is a theme taken up today by another contemporary Geddesian practitioner, this time in planning – Arindam Dutta. Dutta traces this impulse towards organicism and offers an alternative pantheon of organicism at the centre of which is Geddes, but which also includes Immanuel Kant, Johann Wolfgang von Goethe, Augustin

Cournot, John Ruskin, William Whewell, Leon Walras, Alfred Marshall, William Stanley Jevons, Camillo Sitte, Rabindranath Tagore, Prasanta Chandra Mahalanobis, Nandalal Bose and Amartya Sen. Dutta writes:

> This list may well terrify you, incite you to put down this book, and it certainly terrifies me. But what I have here is a rather simple *eidolon* (this is a lovely word, since it indicates both a phantom, an apparition, and the image of an ideal) that I plan to trace across the breadth of modern thought, and that eidolon is the 'curve' as the diagram of the vagaries of human intention.

Geddes's work in Cyprus may be part of this curve, though I suspect it is a crude and early rendering rather than a simple and true arc. It is a much understudied area of his work. Yet it is arguably his largest-scale overseas intervention. A small battered pamphlet, *Cyprus and its Power to Help the East* by Mr and Mrs Patrick Geddes (1897), resides at the National Library of Scotland in Edinburgh. The pamphlet states:

> At the international conference on Armenian Aid, held in London on May 19th/20th 1897, the following resolutions were, amongst others accepted:

> - 'That the present condition of the Armenian people urgently calls for further efforts for the relief of distress and the rebuilding of their social life.'

> - 'That the development of the island of Cyprus as a centre of industrial training in agriculture and manufacture is recommended, and that this conference looks with special interest on the question of silk culture.'

Geddes further stated that:

> We went out to Cyprus on our own account, and not as representatives of any organisation, as we judged it well to refrain from asking or taking any considerable amount of capital, until

we had made sure from personal observation whether Cyprus represented favourable conditions for the starting of agricultural and industrial enterprises.

With the financial backing of £300 from 'two personal friends' and a guarantee of £100 by the Committee of Armenian Refugees fund, they departed for a three month stay. What followed was a typically Geddesian adventure following practices and a repertoire of tools that many will be familiar with, and an emphasis on self-sufficiency. The mix of cultural renewal and practical agriculture and gardening were laid out on a large scale.

They identified deforestation as a major problem, but one of many in the region:

> In agriculture it is not too much to say that almost every conceivable mistake is made, every sin of omission and commission, and the field for improvement is thus correspondingly great.

If de- and indeed re-forestation were central to Geddes's plans for renewal in Cyprus, so was water. He writes:

> Opened up mountain springs which had sealed themselves up with thick deposits of carbonate of lime. Satisfied companions of the trick – here, as often elsewhere, modern science is but recovering the knowledge and the practical wisdom of the East, and that here at their disposal is the very miracle of Moses's rod; for the geological agriculturist has again but to smite the rock in the right place, and the waters gush forth as of old.

Here was Geddes at his theatrical and integrative best, moulding classical storytelling with practical irrigation, inspiring others – as the account goes on to tell – by touring the arid land with a group and then, much like the Biblical prophet he refers to, unblocking old springs and letting the water out.

This literal awakening of the *spirit of place* is remarkable and if the success or failure of the Cyprus project cannot be fully adjudged here, its scale, ambition and imagination were precursors to his future work and an inspiration to ours. On water, Geddes is clear:

Thus even the highest association of Water, as with Peace & Life in the highest sense, are seen to have arisen from their elemental and literal association – that constant normal association of irrigation and intensive agriculture, not only with internal social order, and with individual and general moral progress, which is the vital history of the east; and this whether we read it in the Biblical descriptions of Eden or Palestine, from the literature of Ancient Egypt or from the teaching of Confucius. 'Il faut cultiver notre jardin.'

It is a breathtaking span but three clear lessons spring forth like a newly-cleared water source. First, Spirit is essential. Second, he was aware of Confucius. Third, the constant refrain is place, this time expressed as the exhortation to cultivate our gardens, not turning our backs on the big issues, but at once a symbol of the need to nurture ourselves and a practical literal direction.

There are three primary figures in whom we can discern the influence of Geddes as his ideas travel south and east, borne on the currents of internationalism into the port of Civics and Urbanism, to Italy. These are the architects Giancarlo de Carlo and Gian Carlo Magnoli, and the urban theorist Alberto Magnaghi.

A standard-bearer for Geddes in Italy for many decades was Giancarlo de Carlo (1919–2005) who sadly passed away last year. In his obituary to de Carlo, the great Italian architect Peter Davey wrote:

> As a young man, he was a member of the Resistance against Fascism and the post 1943 Nazi occupation. His first book (published in 1947) was on William Morris, an idealist he revered for his marriage of political commitment and artistic activity. There are wonderful photographs taken just after the War of him passionately addressing workers' meetings in early forms of user participation. Politically aware de Carlo may have been, but he refused to become part of the corrupt Italian web that has entangled architecture, political patronage and officialdom, guaranteeing the mediocrity of so much contemporary architecture. He had no personal style (and thought little of those who have) but approached each new project freshly, seeking input

from site, topography and users. Yet he was never a pasticheur
and remained a committed Modernist. He saw architecture as
part of a continuum of design activity and thinking that
ranged from regional and urban planning to furniture.

De Carlo was the last surviving member of Team x, the group of
young architects set up to organise the tenth CIAM conference in 1956,
and to re-inject social idealism and planetary consciousness into a
Modern Movement that was becoming increasingly moribund. He
would go on to become one of Europe's leading and most inspira-
tional figures.

Geddes's generalism was an inspiration for architects everywhere
seeking unifying theories to view the world, de Carlo said:

Here in Scotland, in Scottish culture... you have one educational pillar which is very important. It is what you call generalism... Specialisation, specialists, I consider in a way to be an
accident of our present time. I think we should go back to the
idea of the general view, and in Scotland you have a good
grounding in this approach not least because of the work of
Patrick Geddes.

Geddes's anarchist roots were also a draw for de Carlo and the
political element of Geddes's work is expressed and explored in the
work of Alberto Magnaghi (of whom more later). But another signif-
icant Italian convert to Geddesian practice and vision is Gian Carlo
Magnoli, who first started his study with his Master's dissertation –
'A flexible method in town planning as seen through the ideas of
Patrick Geddes' (1995) – which he wrote in Architecture and Town
Planning at University of Westminster.

Magnoli – who would go on to produce a PhD in sustainable
architecture and urban development before becoming an architect
and co-designer of The MIT Home of the Future – is fast becoming a
force for innovation and sustainable living. His focus on sustainable
buildings as a learning tool for local communities is directly Geddes
inspired. His ideas have found expression and application not only in
his native Italy but through his work in Greece, Egypt and America.

More recently his design of a 'Smart Village' in Egypt, which utilised renewable energies and was built with recycled materials, won great plaudits and points the way forward in innovative collaborative planning models. As Magnoli put it:

> The disposition of public spaces and the flexible organization of different functions are conceived in order to stimulate social sustainability, allowing the community to be interdependent as much as an ecosystem.
>
> As in any ecosystem, a fractal, coherent, continuous fluctuation at every scale of the system is vital, and this kinetic flexibility is achieved at four levels: 1) decentralized urban planning; 2) reconfigurable spaces; 3) modular building blocks; 4) kinetic structures that respond to light, climate and people.

If we are looking for authentic Geddesian practice today, this is it; inspiring and leading a latent 'responsive architecture' movement.

But even more than de Carlo and Magnoli, another Italian who has been inspired by Geddes is Alberto Magnaghi, founder of the Italian Territorialist School and author of the recent classic *The Urban Village*, a charter for democracy and local self-sustainable development, in which he writes: 'The *territorio* (or region) is a work of art: arguably the highest that humanity has ever produced.'

The Territorialist School is working on the theme of local development at a time when town planning theory is being revised. It is heading towards the replacement of functionalist paradigms which consider the territory as a space, capable of assuming any value only in terms of the economic transformation which it supports. The theoretical aims of the school are:

- definition of a *planning theory* which gives real value to the local identity of the territory, within the sphere of the theoretical model of 'self-sustainable local development';
- the *relationship between local and global* in a socio-economic context which is experiencing rapid evolution;
- definition of *social players*, in an urban and territorial context, as energies which can be deployed in a project and give value to *local identity*, through models of *interactive planning*;

- definition of the *relationship between identity and differences* in a local context (collaboration to establish a local community).

In reviewing the book, Edward Goldsmith quotes the American Wendell Berry:

> If we speak of a healthy community we cannot be speaking of a community that is only human. We are talking about a neigh-bourhood of humans plus the place itself: its soil, its water, its air and all the families and tribes of the non-human creatures that belong to it... if this community is healthy, it is likely to be sustainable, largely self-sufficient and free of tyranny. This means that it is they and not the central government that must control the land, the forests, the rivers and the seas, from which specific communities derive their sustenance.

Alberto Magnaghi's work is exceptional and inspiring. *The Urban Village* is his first book to be published in English. It is the culmination of many years' labour which formed the basis of a *Charter for the New Municipium*, which was presented at the World Social Forum in Porto Alegre in 2002. This has gone on to give birth to a network of civic associations and thinkers promoting these ideas.

Magnaghi's vision is emergent but clear:

> In the conceptual shift from the urban ecosystem to the terri-torial ecosystem, the analytical and planning emphasis is on the fact that each city is generated by its own territory, and also regenerated by its bioregion (Geddes and Mumford).

He goes on:

> We must therefore redesign the virtuous relationship between the city and its territorial and environmental heritage. The virtuous relationship becomes the regenerating source of abandoned and destroyed energies.

The History of a Brook

In creating this important book, Magnaghi is re-embracing the mislaid element of Geddes's thinking – the participatory politics – and uniting it with another thread of current 'bright green thinking', that of bioregionalism, which itself can be traced back to Reclus's *L'histoire d'un ruisseau*.

Consciousness of place and the simple process of making decisions about that place is the red thread that runs through these innovators' minds today. If we ask ourselves why Geddes has a continued influence, it is because he brings an integrative approach to the table where previously there was none and because the collection of key Geddesian themes – geo-technics, democracy, cultural renewal and civics – provides the keys to ecological survival.

On arriving in Yamaguchi in Southern Japan 150 years after Geddes's birth, the participants from Scotland were faced with refreshing green tea served in front of what looked like (and was) a cut-down working recreation of the Camera Obscura from the Outlook Tower.

Japan was intended to be the main topic of this essay but it has taken some time to return to Ueno Park in Tokyo. I started clumsily with my own misapprehension that interest in Geddes must have derived from a post-war need for urban renewal, perhaps a legacy of Japanese experience of earthquakes – such as the huge Kanto Dai-Shinsaiâ Tokyo quake of 1923 – a vague notion that something of Geddes's own approach may have appealed – perhaps his holism and his efforts towards what he called sympathy (or empathy) – to elements of Japanese cultural outlook. Finally I wondered if a path could be discerned between Geddes in India and Geddes in Japan. I was wrong on almost all counts.

So how did we end up listening to 'Auld Lang Syne' on the tannoy in Tokyo?

What was revealed by our friend and colleague Toshihiko Andoh was first that what had inspired Japanese interest in Geddes was his wider focus on *place*, a subject that it would be a fair old understatement to say the Japanese take much more seriously than we do. Indeed, the sensitivity to place at the very most sensitive scale is embedded in Japanese culture, religion and everyday life.

Andoh would explore the links with Geddes since the Meiji period. First of all the notion that Japanese interest in Geddes grew out of earthquake disasters is largely incorrect. Actually the Japanese Ministry of Construction introduced the German system of planning to rebuild Tokyo just after the earthquake in 1923, which killed nearly a hundred thousand people.

Professor Andoh writes:

Generally speaking, those who got interests in Geddes have been the intellectuals who searched for another way of modernization or urbanization. For example, Nakagawa, the secretary of Home Office who wrote a letter to Geddes in 1909, was a member of a Home Office research team on the garden city movement which searched for a more balanced way of urbanization for the local governments. Perhaps he found Geddes' *City Development* during that research?

Andoh again:

The social scientists such as Odauchi and Suzuki searched for the third way of modernization or development. After the 'opening out to the world' in 1868, the Japanese intellectuals had been eager to introduce the Western thought of modernization and been very much influenced by two types of thought. One was liberalism and the other was Marxism. These were very influential, but there had been always one big problem, the gap between these theories and the everyday life of Japanese people. Odauchi and Suzuki were much interested in this topic and searched for more empirical way of social research. This is why they thought Geddes's regional survey very useful.

Soon after the earthquake Shinpei Goto, Minister of Home Affairs, began to reconstruct Tokyo city based on the new town planning planned by the young Japanese engineers. However, it looks as if the Patrick Geddes Idea is not reflected in it, unfortunately.

What was clear to the delegates from Scotland was that something in Geddes's approach chimes with a Japanese cultural sensibility, something perhaps to do with a shared emphasis on harmony, holism and empathy.

Professor Sadakata, a Professor of Geography, was one of the main organisers of the Yamaguchi event, and has helped discern some of the history of Geddes's arrival in Japan:

> Michitoshi Odauchi, human geographer out of office, introduced the idea of Patrick Geddes and applied it for his regional studies around 1930. I think he is the first Japanese who referred to Patrick Geddes in detail. But he did not develop the Patrick Geddes idea further as German ideas began to have a stronger influence.

It would be easy to overplay the importance of Geddes in Japan. At first only the architects and city planners knew his name because Prof I. Nishimura, an architect, translated *Cities in Evolution*. Now, through the work of Dr Ando, Dr Sato and Profs Okutstu and Sadakata, the interest is small but appropriately cross-disciplinary, in fissures and fragments of town planning, localist movements and groups engaged in cultural renewal and artistic expression.

Certain elements remain constant in practice inspired by Geddes. They tend to happen in the cracks-between, where the state withdraws or is shunted aside. This is true in Edinburgh or Yamaguchi, in Falkland or in Florence.

Sadakata writes:

> In recent Japan many local communities try to create the activity to encourage the artistic and cultural event called Machi-Okoshia. The local communities are imposed to reconstruct their own economic base and cultural identity because the central government is now reducing any type financial support for the local communities. The resources such as greenery landscape, the ecological environment, the historical monuments etc. attractive for the people living in the large cities are the key points for the local communities. But in many cases the people in the local communities do not have any basic concept or any idea of their activities. This is the circumstance of the present Japan.

It is unsurprising that interest in Geddes's work has arisen in the space between liberalism and Marxism and 'the gap between these theories and the everyday life'. Neither should it be surprising that the local experience has universal interest, nor that in our world of increasing monoculture and bystander behaviour an expression of fecundity through participation and new forces of vitalism should be appealing. Perhaps what is encouraging is that we now have what one contributor in Yamaguchi called 'a thousand Geddeses' in countries across the world. We will need them.

Bengal Boats and Rickshaw Roads

Kenny Munro

'My childhood river will always be for me my main impulse of the life-stream and of the cosmos'.

PATRICK GEDDES

I WAS UNWITTINGLY INTRODUCED to the influence of Geddes in 1976, while attending a summer school run by one of his students, Philip Boardman, whom I met in Oslo. After graduating as a sculptor, from Edinburgh College of Art in the following year, I sensed there was a renewed role for practising artists in the public domain. I began searching for inspiration to help focus this fresh direction. Initial practical experience in Livingston New Town and creating early work for Ian Hamilton Finlay revealed the broad extremes of client/artist relationships.

The publication of *The Worlds of Patrick Geddes* by Philip Boardman in 1978 provided a timely bridge for redefining the kaleidoscopic world of Geddes. My understanding of the role of the artist as a catalyst within communities and the public domain was given a new perspective. Exhibitions in Edinburgh during the 1980s further endorsed for me Sir Patrick Geddes and his work. The spirit of his work revealed the interrelatedness of the world, giving it a fresh and stimulating creative structure, grounded on democratic principles, encouraging, and indeed promoting, a sense of challenging enquiry. There was a passion for respecting the potential of life in every form.

I wholeheartedly identified with this philosophy, which provided the spur for much of my own work: seeking to reinforce the practical role of the arts as an essential component within all communities and more than a so-called 'luxury'. The motto *Creando Pensamus*, By Creating We Think, offers a praxis and prescient aspiration for many to follow.

I connected again with the work of Boardman and his family in Montpellier, where they had redrawn a layout map of Geddes's Scots College and symbolic gardens in line with how Boardman remembered the place in the 1920s. Built on a high rocky outcrop, with a panoptic tower overlooking the ancient city of Moorish science and antiquity, with the oldest botanical garden in Europe at its core, this clearly provided an ideal location for creative thinking. Geddes laid out gardens and grottos as a method of teaching students and a practical expression of his beliefs. The global vision was expanded with the building of the Indian College on the same site, but the ambition to build an American College, which Lewis Mumford might have helped administer, was never realised. (Walter Stephen's essay 'Cartoons by Hendrik Willem Van Loon: Geddes, Van Loon and Mumford' in this volume sheds some light on why this could never have happened.)

Such was my curiosity that I travelled to Montpellier between 1990 and 1998 with fellow artist Lesley-May Miller. We spent a total of about ten months in the region over that period, collaborating with artists and academics as we wrestled with how best to revitalise the spirit of the Collège des Écossais and what we should or could do with its symbolic gardens and the deteriorating bas-relief sculptures on the building.

Demanding a Greater Public Profile for Creative Expression

One of the strongest examples of collaborative 'public sculpture' from this period, applying the rigour of the arts as a new political and practical expression of *Creando Pensamus*, was the 'Niches Project', Edinburgh, 1991. The historic stone niches of the northern wall of Waterloo Place were 'creatively kidnapped' to house an exciting and innovative outdoor gallery, promoted by Edinburgh Sculpture Workshop. Each of the ten niches, on the north wall, was utilised to accommodate galvanised steel art cabinets, glazed with clear polycarbonate and housing diverse creative contributions from across Scotland.

My contribution was to reflect the spirit of the Outlook Tower, in collaboration with Murdo Macdonald, George Wyllie and Stan Bonnar. A Geddes 'thinking machine' started with a grid of squares which were filled with key words and ideas as they related to each other. In our 'Niche Project' a series of compartments within a cabinet were filled with carefully chosen objects to become, in effect, a three-dimensional thinking machine. Other niches held contributions from individuals, art student groups and schools.

A unique venture, the Niches Project was considered a success, coinciding with the innovative 'Lux Europa' initiative, illuminating the city with lightworks, and was further promoted with concepts such as 'The City is a Work of Art' by the Scottish Sculpture Trust.

There was much public debate and the project coincided with the growing public demand for more devolved powers for Scotland. Significantly, the cabinets were not vandalised and remained intact for the agreed period of about three months. The public seemed to approve.

Research trips, with British Council support, promoted touring art shows to and from Montpellier, and added energy to the Franco-Scottish exchange. Outcomes included temporary neon displays of the triad Place, Work, Folk, photographed in dialogue with nature. We displayed a prototype arts cabinet, a form of vitrine, at Maison d'Écosse in 1993. Later that year French artists brought their work to Edinburgh, showing a compilation of eclectic sculpture, video, neon and painting at the annual exhibition of the Society of Scottish Artists. A version of the Arts Cabinet – a compilation of symbols, text and publications within nine clear perspex boxes, held in a stainless steel frame – was permanently installed in the Geddes College, Montpellier in 1998.

I have a curious memory from that period. Architect Graham Ross visited the Jardin des Plantes in Montpellier, following his research on Geddes and the association with botanist Flahault. His detective work paid off with the discovery of various papers in an archive, some of which had been published in Scotland and annotated by Geddes. I was pleased to receive copies of these.

At the time I was looking for encouragement for a schools project to enable a creative exploration of the River Forth, from source to sea. On the front cover of one of the historic leaflets, relating to outdoor pursuits for a summer school programme conducted in the late 19th century at Ramsay Garden, Geddes had hand written: 'Turn to page nine.' So I did. And in doing so I was astonished to discover, as if personally directed, his particular interests in the River Forth and the excursion he had conducted, over 100 years before! Yet another example of the kind of thing quoted by James Mackinnon:

> The Greek epigram on Plato is applicable to him – wherever I go in my mind, I meet Geddes coming back.

A Creative Journey:
From Montpellier to Kolkata via Auckland

Much has been written about Geddes's life and achievements. In this essay I wish to concentrate on his real practical legacy, which we can still benefit from today. The energy and appetite with which Geddes explored 'human geography' was to some extent predetermined by the great lineage of surveyors, geologists and plant collectors in Scotland. Symbols abound which focus our understanding of how our ancestors perceived the world. For example, a free standing multifacetted stone sundial at the west end of the Royal Museum of Scotland reveals the passionate interest which Scots in the 18th century had for their international affairs. On a tall elegant stone pillar, the name 'Bengal' is carved in noble script close to an ornamental gnomon. probably a laird in Invernesshire was keen on both chronology and his trading interests close to the Ganges. How many more physical reminders of India remain undiscovered?

To be reminded of the centuries during which the Scots travailled in Bengal, one need only visit the profoundly interesting Scottish Cemetery in the middle of Kolkata, which reveals an exotic tableau of Celtic crosses mixed with Moghul style structures in rendered brick. One can read about the extreme opulence of jute and coal barons, and the desperately sad deaths of children and young adults who had spent only a matter of months in the Raj.

Significantly, although at a much later period, Anna Morton died in Calcutta in 1916. She succumbed to enteric fever while valiantly supporting her husband Geddes.

In 1999 I learned that Aberdeenshire local authority was inviting proposals to help promote and activate a fresh arts policy within the region. I suggested that a creative engagement with the town of Ballater should be considered. The enthusiasm locally was such that a group was constituted as The Geddes Ballater Group 2004. Their primary objective was to help raise awareness of Geddes in Ballater, as well as to support international plans for the 150th anniversary of his birth in 2004.

I travelled to Auckland in 2000, with support from the Geddes Memorial Trust, to meet descendant Alex Geddes, who has a marvellous archive of family papers including e-mail transcripts of letters sent back to Perth in the 1860s, as well as an array of books, sketches, a clock from Mount Tabor in Perth and letters hand-written by PG on letter-headed paper from the Scots College.

Rather than simply celebrating the historic links, the ambitions of the Group have been, and continue to be, driven by the contemporary significance of Geddes and his philosophy:

He believed it essential that people first appreciate themselves and their place, and then look beyond to other people, cultures, languages, religions and international regions.

In a practical sense this is being realised with local and international projects, such as 'Language of Rivers and Leaves' 2004 and the current project, 'Song of the Rickshaw' 2005–2007. These promote reciprocal exchanges, raise cultural awareness, and involve schools and communities in both countries.

Physical outcomes which can be seen in Ballater, since 1999, include carved timber sculpture markers by Gavin Smith, which display drawings etched on stainless steel by school pupils. Tree planting, a Geddes Gate (in wrought iron and copper) for Ballater Primary School, interpretation panels in a 'concept bus shelter' on the main road and a historic bronze portrait of Geddes and exhibition in the Library build up to ensure a real contemporary Geddes presence in the town of his birth.

To complement the plans for the anniversary celebration in 2004, Tom Potter designed a splendid exhibition linked to a comprehensive website.

Drawn by the magnetism of the global activities of Sir Patrick Geddes and the work and research undertaken by members of his family, I made my first field trip to India in 2002. After initial contact with Bengal there followed train journeys to the temple of Konark in Orissa, and an inspiring journey north to Darjeeling. I learned about Rabindranath Tagore, the Bengali sage/poet/artist and winner of the Nobel Prize for Literature, who made a significant impact on the cultural climate of Europe in the early 20th century. The Tagore college at Shanteniketan provided an educational/philosophical model for continuing Geddes's work and partly inspired the establishment of the Collège des Écossais. Teaching by practical example, working outdoors under trees, the holistic approach is appropriately symbolised when students graduate and receive their formal certificate in the form of a leaf.

Discovering the Energy of the School of Art and Craft, Kolkata

I went on to stay with the artists who ran a small specialised art school in Asgar Mistri Lane, Kolkata, beside an open public space called Sibtala Math. High palm trees, kids playing cricket, tanners laying out dyed skins to dry and the shrill cry of hawks circling the sky set the mood. The school of about 100 students (ages 4–18) specialises in developing creative skills in drawing, painting, sculpture and the performing arts. It was interesting to note that the school does not deal with religious matters and proclaims 'We have no religion'. The students conduct their daily studies in local state schools, returning in the evenings and at weekends for their art tuition. I was most impressed by their creative confidence, energy and ability to communicate well in English.

The School of Art and Craft has been established for over 20 years and, although run on very meagre means, it has been successful in propelling many young men and women into professional arts careers and regularly promotes multi-arts festivals. The board of directors, comprising politicians, parents and academics, helps guide the policies and long term objectives.

Bengal Boat to Ballater

Since 2002, creative links have intensified between us and Tandra Chandra, Pulak Goshe and the students of the School of Art and Craft. Tandra visited Scotland in 2003 and was introduced to the Ballater Geddes Group. Their plan to celebrate the 150th anniversary of PG's birth in 2004 took shape as part of a growing national and international programme. Importantly, this seed of the reciprocal project was given practical form and focus as an educational event by using a Bengal river boat as an icon to illustrate the ongoing significance of rivers and our dependency on water.

This provided the framework for a creative ecological study, involving school pupils in interpreting themes through art, music, poetry contrasting and comparing river communities in both countries. Together we galvanised an exercise in global social awareness, citizenship and cultural diversity. Surely Geddes would have been delighted to see how the Valley Section was being stretched and tweaked into a total educational experience.

We visited a boat yard at Balaghore, sited among bamboo groves near the banks of the Hooghly river, where the commissioned 18-foot craft was built. Apart from the hum of a distant bandsaw, the sight of clusters of boats being worked on, in various states of construction, might have been the same for 500 years. Only manual tools and techniques were to be seen. Carvel-formed hulls of beautiful simplicity were held fast by rope and leather tourniquets while large iron staples crimped the planks together as they were formed around the keel. The hulls of sea boats are often stitched together with rope, as seen on the beach at Puri, but in this yard they used galvanised staples to guard against the corrosive properties of sea water.

All the planking and thwarts were planed to shape and gauged by eye. Simple timber wedges and staves held the curved panels at the correct rising pitch of the hull as they were fixed in place. Spindle drills pierced the boat timbers before nailing and stapling commenced. The men sat and held the drill bits in alignment with their toes as they performed the task of drilling the ribs.

The long hand-crafted nails were driven through planks and ribs then clenched and bent over on the inside with the confident attack of a heavy hammer. Tar is normally applied to the hull of Indian boats but we wanted ours left with untreated wood for the school's painting programme.

Seeing this construction process reminded me of the boat yards that used to exist around Britain and made me think of the local yards on the Forth, such as Aitkens in Fife and Weatherheads in East Lothian. It reminded me also that the Valley Section is merely a model; the activities in it are not frozen in time, but change as society or the environment or the price of copper changes.

On completion, the boat had the most bizarre journey and introduction to Kolkata. The boat yard was some 30 kilometres from the school and the boat was transported at night, strapped onto a tricycle rickshaw. Two men took turns pedalling. This, I should say, was not at our request but was the solution which the boat yard chose for moving the precious vessel. I had thought about asking the obvious question as the yard was so close to the Hooghly...

Sonar Tari (Golden Boat) was inspired by Rabindranath Tagore's poem of the same name. After its extraordinary journey the beautiful craft was set on a bamboo framework, in the garden of the School of Arts and Crafts, and was then painted and decorated by the pupils. Symbols of trees, plants, river life and poetry were gradually painted with great passion onto the curved hull. One evening a cyclone of unimaginable ferocity battered Kolkata and halted us for a few days. Luckily the boat wasn't damaged by falling trees and we were able to complete the painting and preparations for the public procession (PLATE 2B).

A pageant with children, parents and community, led by local bagpipers and escorted by a few police, took us on a circuit round the locality. A radio commentator sat in the first float, explaining the project in Bengali and English for all who were interested. In the evening, a programme of song and dance culminated with speeches on the historic and contemporary links with Scotland, including issues as diverse as eco-tourism and the education system in India. Geddes would have loved it – especially the pipers! Remember the grainy photograph of Alasdair leading the children of Castlehill School down to their new community garden?

During the following month the boat was filled with models, flutes, masks and paintings created by the children and crated and shipped to Scotland, via Colombo.

Bengal Boat Arrives in Scotland:
A Journey Completed by Juggernaut and Tractor!

A programme of creative exchange brought Bengali and Scottish artists together enabling Aberdeenshire communities and pupils to experience and take part in the Indian art workshops – music, dance and model boat making – all focusing around the 150th anniversary events. Tandra Chanda and Pulak Goshe, the directors of the Kolkata school, were formally invited by Aberdeenshire Council and undertook a broad range of workshops with a broad cross-section of communities in the North East.

On 2 October (a birthday which Geddes shared with Mahatma Gandhi), a pageant with pipers led a procession at Ballater and Finzean with a symbolic launch of *Sonar Tari* on Loch Kinord (PLATE 3A). The boat was baptised and, despite jets of water gradually filling the vessel through the dry timbers, Pulak and I were able to navigate Indian wood on Scottish water. Rowing with the beautifully painted oars, a few hundred metres out from the shore we raised the magnificent red sail, revealing the name of the craft in Bengali script – *Sonar Tari*.

A great sense of achievement was shared by the crowd on the shore, including a film crew. The boat was then displayed for a month in the Alford Transport Museum, becoming the most popular exhibit for school drawing classes.

Scottish Parliament: December 2004

As a fantastic and fitting conclusion to the 'Language of Rivers and Leaves' project we were, with significant help from Robin Harper MSP, invited to present a show case of the Ballater Group's exhibition and pupils' achievements at the Lobby Garden gallery in the Parliament at Holyrood. A formal launch was held – not with the Bengal boat, unfortunately – which was well attended by officials and a bus load of Aberdeenshire school pupils. A significant impact was made and Mike Rumbles MSP from Aberdeenshire supported the event. A paper was presented to the Parliament by Robin Harper, formally registering the ongoing significance of the philosophy promoted by Sir Patrick Geddes.

The boat *Sonar Tari* is now in 'dry dock' at the Scottish Maritime

Museum, Irvine, where one can also view the video which captured the mood of events in both countries.

Song of the Rickshaw: A Paradigm for Sustainable Transport? October 2005

The monsoon lasted longer than expected in Kolkata and I recognised the determined 'Scottish' rain which fell for hours on the small art school garden at Shibtala Math. Ironically, on one of the many ancient cast iron water fonts in the city, an embossed motto reads: 'Waste not Want not' – a statement which might have been instigated by a Presbyterian water engineer. So profound now in the 21st century...

Temperatures of 35°C and 100 per cent humidity are rarely recorded in Edinburgh or Ballater. But this was glorious India and my third visit to Bengal in three years. On this trip I experienced the extraordinary festival venerating the Hindu goddess Durga. Thousands of temporary shrines are created housing ornate multi-armed deities, made with clay on a bamboo frame. Commissioned annually from local artists, they are gloriously painted and festooned with rich fabric and reflective foil. Many of these sculptures are housed within monumental timber and papier maché replicas of historic temples (*pandels*).

On specific days, in seemingly endless procession, thousands of these artworks, some three metres in height, are moved by truck, ox-cart and rickshaw to the banks of the Hooghly, where teams of young men struggle and strain to carry the sculptures to the water's edge for immersion and dispersal.

The event is cleansing, liberating and very much in the spirit of Hindu philosophy; celebrating birth, death and renewal by uniting with the Hooghly river as part of the mighty Ganges. On an economic level, this annual creative ritual also ensures that artists and crafts people have a cyclical series of commissions every year. The clay and bamboo sculptures are left to float away or sink, biodegrading to mix with silt, clay and the ashes of human remains; all eventually recycled as the *chakra* of life.

It worried me to see some recent figures of Durga made in fibreglass, presenting a real threat to sustainable art which could undermine aspects of the Hindu philosophy. The ancient tradition connecting with rivers continues, and these public celebrations made me think: What spiritual links do we in the West have with our landscape and rivers? Scotland can rediscover her rivers by observing these great Indian traditions.

The fabulous and somewhat chaotic festival atmosphere in Kolkata created the backdrop for the origination of the project 'Song of the Rickshaw'.

The success of the 'Bengal Boat' project provided confidence and inspired a new creative response to the question of eco-friendly transport. In a similar vein, we were now to focus on the significance of two- and three-wheeled rickshaw transportation in Kolkata and how it could inform the development of non-polluting transport in Scotland. Will it survive in a city which has a population almost twice that of all Scotland?

Ironically, the Indian press was reporting that local government was, yet again, considering the decommissioning of the two-wheeled, hand-pulled rickshaw. A very topical and controversial matter which some might say is an issue of exploitation of human rights – how can we reconcile the question of human labour; men pulling or pedalling heavy loads and passengers around in all weathers with little thanks and even less payment?

This and other questions were addressed by 80 students at the art school. Within the general scope of examining the cultural associations between India and Scotland, we also discussed the trading links and the many plants and trees which became of key importance to the UK economy. Such as the massive growth of the tea, spice and jute industries and the less well known importation of *cutch* tree resin for the preservation of fishing boat gear (tanning/barking sheds can still be seen on the island of Arran). The issues of deforestation are also of current concern for India. But this is not a new challenge – it was reported upon by the British Forestry Association in 1850 and from this the Indian Forest School was established at Derha Dun, in the Himalayas, in 1878. In Geddes's time it was still a major issue. One of the reasons for Geddes's lack of enthusiasm for Gandhi was the latter's failure to grasp the forestry problem.

Flash floods and waterlogging are a seasonal reality in Bengal. People cope and adapt well. But they presented serious challenges when conducting the outdoor work with the School of Art and Craft at Asgar Mistri Lane. Temporary covered areas were made to protect the rickshaws and to enable painting in the evening. Many young hands worked by light from dangling electric bulbs and squirmed, in the wet, to avoid the hungry mosquitoes.

Two rickshaws were procured and purchased. The painting and decorating were completed, despite the wet weather. The pupils adopted the powerful traditions of Kalighat painting and wood block printing to influence their designs, featuring birds, fish and Indian gods. They were meticulously painted using powerful graphic treatments and vibrant colours. Floral patterns and leaf designs were applied to the timber bearers and metal chassis. Outlines were drawn around small feet and these 'carbon' footprints were painted in bright colours onto the footplates of both vehicles.

Model rickshaws were created, and larger painted wooden panels enabled individual students the opportunity to excel by interpreting contemporary scenes of street life in what was once considered to be the Second City of the Empire.

All these endeavours were prefocussed on a public procession in Kolkata on 2 November, followed by an evening exhibition and seminar. Preparations for the procession were extensive. The decorated rickshaws were elevated to the status of artworks and lifted onto bamboo trailers with truck axles. The pupils, parents and community assembled to form a human chain, with brightly coloured flags and saris. All were led by a colourful Bengali Pipe Band. The energy and creative exuberance was awesome and make me feel confident in saying that Patrick Geddes's love of pageant, involving folk and communicating ideas, was surely driven by his passion for India and its festival-fuelled culture.

In the evening the Mayor of Kolkata attended the exhibition and performance of song and dance. A unique song was composed specially for the project and sung that night. Representatives from local government and the Professor of Botany talked at length about Scotland's relationship with India and the ongoing significance of sustainable agriculture, fishing and forestry.

As with the Golden Boat (Sonar Tari) in 2004, the project was not completed until the Scottish linkage had been made. In May 2006 the rickshaws and their associated artefacts were shipped to Scotland and a programme of activities with Scottish schools was organised, involving the Ballater Geddes Group.

Tandra Chanda and Pulka Ghosh have been given a prestigious commission by the British Council. They are to creatively direct the work of eight Indian schools which are collaborating with river community schools by the Thames in London and the Yangtse, Chonquing, China.

> The process of planning is like a complicated and never finished game of chess... in both, you have to study existing situations carefully before making any move and then try to turn difficulties into opportunities.

So said Geddes, who believed that the arts provided a vital element of community life, offering a way of involving people and enriching their lives. His work as an ecologist and botanist led to an interest and care for the natural and urban environment and his campaigning work to promote cultural diversity continues to be important today.

Art, too often in the West, is packaged into halls and galleries. The innovative regeneration of rural and urban space has the capacity to expand the way we think about the evolving role of arts in the community, art of the outdoors, and the needs and values which local citizens and visitors bring to such locations.

More outdoor creativity is needed, both to inspire and to provide essential skills for constructive engagements in our world. We need, too, a philosophy of creative fieldwork; whether teamworking to form an outdoor classroom, making a spiritual pilgrimage across the hills or sailing through the magical islands of the West Coast.

Practical exploration, engaging with aquascape/landscape, outdoor education and creative holistic training are sustainable ways forward; certainly in terms of understanding our place in the cosmos.

I believe some of this humanitarian work provides not an easy solution, but a key for unlocking the potential in each individual and community. Taking responsibility for cause and effect in the ever-changing cultural landscape is a creative quest. It is not a simple solution or necessarily likely to make one popular.

However 'the creative irritant' as a catalyst for change is a positive force. And, as the oyster can organically generate a natural form of perceived beauty by addressing a challenge, so too can we 'try to turn difficulties into opportunities'.

Let us remember Thoreau:

If a man does not keep pace with his companions, perhaps it is because he hears a different drummer. Let him step to the music which he hears; however measured or far away.

Overkill

Frank Spaven

Introduction

IN 1998, HARPERCOLLINS held a competition to find one word that summed up the 20th century. The winner was *television*, followed by *technology* and then *communication*. My entry was *overkill*, meaning the unrestrained use of new powers of all kinds, in excess of what is necessary and without heeding their wider effects. This thought had first arisen in the mid-1930s, from a lecture by the popular philosopher Professor C.E.M. Joad at Edinburgh University on 'The growing disparity between human power and human wisdom'. Here are some examples that have struck me since then, along with indications of how the disparity may be overcome.

Wars

The primary definition of overkill relates to its origins – the deployment of more destructive weapons, especially nuclear, than is necessary for immediate military advantage. The justification given for the bombing of Hiroshima and Nagasaki in 1945 was that it would prevent heavy Allied casualties in further ground fighting and ensure Japan's early defeat, even though it would mean a massive slaughter of civilians. That has left a legacy forever of the threat of disasters, because of which one of its inventors, Oppenheimer, had opposed its use. Thankfully, the threat of *Mutually Assured Destruction* has deterred the Cold War nations, but like others we still hold on to Trident; and some *rogue* states may still pose threats. Would they be quelled by USA's latest missile proposal or would that lead to another arms race?

In traditional warfare there has usually not been overkill in the above sense. Killing itself, of the armed by the armed, may have to be accepted as the price of a just war for freedom as in 1939–45 – if it does not involve civilians, as it hardly ever did in the Western Desert in 1940–43. But it did in the air battle for Malta in 1942 and it did as soon as the Eighth Army landed in Italy, where the scene changed into two years of Allied air and land assaults on or around villages and towns; and systematic massacres by ss and other units of civilians in the villages where they met any Resistance fighters.

By the end of that War throughout the World, over 30 million civilians had been slaughtered, massacred, starved to death or lost and 24 million military personnel had been killed or gone missing, surely the most appalling overkill in human history.

Is there *any* cure for war-making? It would mean preventing wars from starting, which we signally failed to do by countering any of Hitler's triumphant territorial advances before 1939, but have certainly done politically with the union of neighbouring states in the EU. It would mean ending the practice of adopting any new technology in armaments, even if it is not needed, with its risk that the greater capacity to wage war leads to a greater political willingness to do so, for example, where there are demands for access to essential resources of oil and water in the Middle East. It would certainly mean building up, at long last, a far stronger International Military Force under the UN, on behalf of which or in default of which, British and other troops currently have to do the vital and difficult job of peace keeping, for example in Kosovo and Sierra Leone.

The Earth

Next to wars, the depletion or near exhaustion of the Earth's atmosphere, its natural forests, animals and fisheries, its mineral resources and soils is surely the most damaging and longest established form of overkill. It now continues on virtually a world scale, at the hands of unrestrained, short-term profit seekers, using ever more effective technology and power for exploitation. It certainly is a deadly menace for the future.

There is now little doubt that the world is in for a hard time of climatic and sea-level changes through global warming, mainly caused by pollution of greenhouse gases, nearly all from the wealthy countries, and lower carbon dioxide intake by depleted forests. It is already causing increasingly frequent *natural* disasters in the Third World.

Nearly all the total world consumption of non-renewable oil and mineral resources is by the rich countries (83–94 per cent in 1974–76). *It is obvious that the world cannot afford the USA. Nor can it afford Western Europe or Japan...* Think of it – one American drawing on resources that could sustain 50 Indians! (Schumacher, 1974).

Shared access to and use of resources must include the town and village land where most of us live, even in the Highlands. Its proper use is usually safeguarded by our Town and Country Planning Acts, but in some local authorities, councillors allow over-development, under pressure from commercial firms and yet contrary to their own Local Plan, the advice of their own planning staff and the views of local bodies. In the experience of Inverness Civic Trust, these anti-planning cases have often been supermarkets and supermalls, of which there are now as many as 15.

Fortunately, there is a growing movement in this country to respect our environment, sustain our resources and plan development and conservation as partners, promoted by local authorities under Local Agenda 21 and by bodies like Friends of the Earth, and followed in many excellent school and youth projects.

This new wisdom has to become universal, starting with an understanding of nature as a sacred trust and a new respect for resources, along the lines of John Muir. It will have to be promoted very widely and acted on not only locally but also by governments and multinational companies. To achieve this, Al Gore, Vice-President of the USA, has proposed a global version of the Marshall Plan, the post-War European Recovery Programme.

Riches

In the past century there have been tremendous improvements in general standards of living. An important part of this, in health, has been achieved, with no ill-effects, by the wise use of science and technology in a public service operated by dedicated professional staff. For the rest, although there have been benefits from steadily rising profit-making and private affluence, there have been ill-effects, of two kinds, amounting to overkill.

In the first place, through the virtual worship of material wealth, contrary to all Christian teaching, society is departing from personal and communal wisdom about the good life into an *anything goes* mentality and, for example, a willingness to be pulled by powerful persuaders into more and more consumer spending. In the second place, there is a widening gap between the well-off majority and the poorer, so that in Scotland today one in four adults do not have enough income to take part in normal life. There is no *trickle down effect* from a general private affluence and many public services and benefits on which the poor rely are inadequate.

This gap is huge between the developed North or First World and the developing South or Third World. Of the world's population of 6 billion, a quarter live in relative luxury and another quarter live in a state of malnutrition and widespread ill-health and illiteracy. Many of the not so poor in between are also vulnerable in their recurring emergencies of drought, flooding, famine and civil war. The economy of these countries is held back by the harsh terms of traders for their resources, products and labour and by the failure of most rich governments to help them enough and to carry out the recommendations of the Brandt Commission on International Development.

Recently, the G8 richest nations were again being strongly pressed to cancel the debts of the poorest countries, but with little or no success so far. They do give overseas development aid, but still far below the target level agreed years ago. Our charities, such as Christian Aid and the Intermediate Technology Development Group, help a lot at the grass-roots, in cooperative projects with their partners and in disaster emergencies.

One obvious way of increasing aid to the poor, both at home and abroad, would be to increase and earmark taxation on *fat cats*, polluters and users of scarce resources. Even that would no doubt need strong public pressure on governments. Another way for us personally would be to opt out of consumerism and waste and revive thrift, learning from our Third World partners how to do it.

May I live simply so that others may simply live.

Cars

Of all the technical innovations of the past century, motor cars and lorries have surely brought the most widespread benefits and at the same time, through persistent over-growth and under-control, the greatest adverse impacts. The problems of collisions, casualties, pollution, using up fuel, congestion, noise, visual intrusion, waste of town space and restriction of other users, are now more often recognised but seldom tackled at the roots. The basic trouble, especially with cars, is the failure to recognise that these machines can be moved freely in any direction at any time, in the hands of an army of amateurs, some of whom, still being human, will inevitably at some time make careless mistakes or break the rules. This situation has never existed and would not be tolerated in any other form of transport.

Education, engineering and enforcement have certainly helped to alleviate this situation (though sadly hardly at all in over-crowded Third World cities). Policies to contain, if not solve it, in Britain are now fortunately on the way to statutes – but will they be drastic enough? In built-up areas there should be a general 20 mph speed limit, with 5–10 mph in home zones and school zones; and in town centres, prohibition of most cars, with park-and-ride, and priority for walkers, then cyclists, buses, taxis and delivery vans (not HGVs, which should transship outwith the town centre).

Between towns and regions, the way people travel and goods are moved must be changed, for example to shift more traffic to rail and sea; and the need for transport reduced by increasing local production and marketing and curbing centralisation of services.

Pressure groups working for these changes, like Transform Scotland and its member organisations, must be strongly supported and those local authorities and towns here and abroad, notably in the Netherlands, that are setting an example, made known.

Communication

The nearly universal means of communication today, by ever faster and more frequent transport of all kinds, ever expanding TV and other media, e-mail, the Internet and mobile phones, all pushed hard by competitors, is surely the most striking example of technology advancing explosively that we have ever had – and it is bringing apparently welcomed benefits. But already we know that the mobiles have unsightly masts and health risks and we hear that managers are being stressed by a flood of information or computer failures, that the young are becoming obsessed by it all and that the media in general and the uncontrolled and unedited Internet in particular are invaded by irrelevant and tabloid material, pornography and fraud.

Even if all this could be sorted out and some restraint introduced, one insidious effect would remain. This is its proponents' triumphant claim of *abolishing distance* and so enabling people to travel, work and think free from ties to any one place, job or community – but without any real appreciation of the people they are now in contact with. At the same time our local functions and identity are being over-run by incoming goods and ideas and the bonds of home and *belonging* to a distinctive place are being weakened by easy means and habits of *going away*. So we may no longer even meet our neighbours and appreciate our own environment just by walking beyond the front gate.

One way of bringing wisdom into this situation, beyond being personally very selective in using these technologies, would be to revive Patrick Geddes's basic ecological principle and regional survey synthesis of Place, Work, Folk, which he developed in different parts of the world. Modern studies of it should be encouraged in schools and universities and examples made known of communities that are succeeding in *not losing place*.

Conclusion

The pervasive menace of overkill has appeared with diverse powers and effects. They all show lack of restraint in uncontrolled hands, in an age of scientific and technical discoveries which are used to excess for private profit in a consumer society. The icons of capitalism must take into account the external costs they impose on people, environment and resources, in a new system of sustainable economics. This will require radical changes in business, government and international policies and joint action to set up a global development programme.

This has been proposed before and is unlikely to happen without our persistent personal support and strong public pressure, along these lines:

- Be committed to a spiritual faith and the fellowship of a like-minded local group.
- Opt out of consumerism and live simply.
- Support pressure groups which campaign to save resources and help the poorest.
- Keep in touch with councillors, MSPs and MPs.
- Vote for a political party committed to these policies, including increased taxation.

Dunbar to Berwick
A special part of the East Coast Main Line

Frank Spaven

THIS 29 MILES of railway is physically quite distinctive. While its first few coastal miles after Dunbar continue its generally straight and level course from Edinburgh, it then has to get through the Lammermuir Hills where they extend right out into the North Sea. It does so by climbing four and a half miles at 1 in 96 up the Cockburnspath Bank, the steepest gradient on the whole East Coast Main Line. It then curves down and criss-crosses the Eye Water valley, comes out past Reston and swings round past Ayton and above Burnmouth onto six miles of

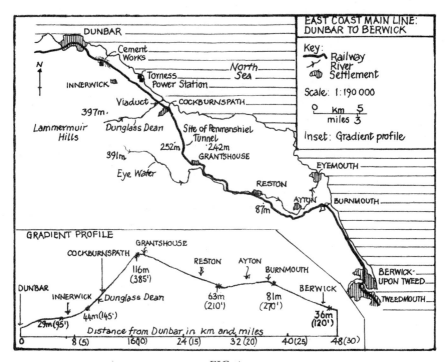

FIG 4

East Coast Main Line: Dunbar to Berwick and Gradient Profile
(Norman Thomson)

cliff-tops to Berwick and then high over the Tweed to Tweedmouth. A few miles further on it resumes its generally straight and level course most of the way to London.

The Cockburnspath Bank is not so severe as others such as Beattock – 10 miles at 1 in 88 to 1 in 69 – but it certainly used to slow down heavy trains, especially goods trains. In and even after steam-hauled days, they often had to have banking assistance from pilot locos at Dunbar. Innerwick Station had a relief siding for through goods trains, to give clearance to express passenger trains climbing the hill.

FIG 5
Innerwick Signal Box. John Mack in command, August 1931
(Frank Spaven)

In 1933, the five-mile section between Co'path and Grantshouse signal boxes was divided into two by automatic colour-light signals half-way up. Today, especially since electrification in 1991, passenger trains, at least, go fast right up the Bank with no bother, and even faster down it. The traveller by rail (or road) hardly notices any difference. Walkers on the Southern Upland Way, which parallels the line on the other side of the Pease Burn valley up to the summit, are more likely to appreciate where they are!

The line has two large masonry viaducts on it – the splendid, land-mark, 28-arch Royal Border Bridge across the Tweed at Berwick

(Robert Stephenson, 1850), and the less well-known viaduct across Dunglass Dean, near Co'path (Grainger and John Miller, 1846). This has a main arch and three arches on each side and stands high, in every sense, above four historic road bridges nearby, of which the newest on the A1, built in 1992, replaced a faulty 1932 structure (PLATE 3B). A very similar, but larger viaduct was also designed by John Miller at Ballochmyle in Ayrshire in 1848 and a long one of 36 arches over the Almond on the Glasgow-Edinburgh line in 1842. That these bridges have lasted so long and so well, carrying heavier, faster and more frequent trains than were ever anticipated, is a remarkable tribute to the companies, the engineers, the contractors and the workmen who built them and have maintained them. (Up to 2,700 men worked on the Royal Border Bridge in 1847–50; one of them was my great grandfather, a young stonemason.) (PLATE 4A)

This railway has had to cope with several disasters. In August 1948, overwhelming floods on the normally quiet Eye Water – with a low rainfall catchment – washed away all seven bridges over it, caused three landslips and, near Ayton, a huge dam-up, and required all trains to be diverted to the Waverley or Carstairs routes for several months – though fewer than expected. A similar event had taken place in 1846 and a lesser version occurred in 1956.

FIG 6
Cockburnspath Bank after 1956 floods.
(Frank Spaven)

In March 1979, Penmanshiel Tunnel near the top of the Bank collapsed, entombing two men who were among those lowering the track
to take higher containers. Was this due in part to the abandonment of
the tunnel by the first contractor building it in 1845, long before a different firm took it over; or – more likely – by the vast flood waters
pouring through it in 1948, plus the instability of the overlying, tilted
Silurian strata? The whole tunnel had to be sealed up and the line
diverted on a curve round the end of the tunnelled spur (PLATE 4B).
Disasters have also been threatened by slippage of the cliff-tops south
of Burnmouth, but averted in time by moving the line further back;
the line was temporarily blocked by a landslide in the heavy rains of
early August 2002.

Another feature of this line is that it has no stations between Dunbar
(pop 6,500) and Berwick (12,000), to serve a nearby population of
about 8,000 along its 28 miles. It used to have seven, including junctions
at Burnmouth for the short branch to Eyemouth, and at Reston (plus
Tweedmouth) for the long link lines into the Borders. They were closed
in the 1950s, or the Beeching era – a drastic thinning out but not the
worst! On the West Coast Main Line over Beattock there are no stations for 47 miles between Carstairs and Lockerbie, where there used
to be seven serving a small rural population, plus branches to Moffat
and through Biggar. By far the worst off, of course, has been the
Waverley Line, which used to serve directly a nearby population of
over 80,000 from 21 stations on its 98 miles through the Borders and
Midlothian.

In a complete contrast of functions and policies, on the North and
West Highland Lines there are 66 halts or stations, three, four or five per
28 miles, available to serve sparse populations, tourists and occasional
small towns along 405 route miles. Along most of the other lines outwith Central Scotland, there are still one, two or three stations per 28
miles. Between Newcastle and Carlisle and then along the coast to
Barrow, there are as many as 38 stations in 147 miles.

The striking feature of changing traffic on the line has been the
disappearance of local trains and railwaymen, with their stations. The
time-honoured 'Berwick Local' from Edinburgh, calling some eight times
a day each way, ceased in 1964, as did the local freight pick-ups then
or later, which had been a valued and thriving link for agriculture,

fishing, coal and local trades for a century, both giving substantial employment at every station – now all gone, ousted by road transport and distant terminals. However, the volume and speed of through traffic have increased. After 1846 there were five passenger trains a day each way, taking three quarters of an hour (non-stop) to one hour and 15 minutes. By 1965 there were 15 a day taking 29–38 minutes and today there are some 25, mostly GNER and a few Virgin, usually taking 24 minutes if they have stopped at Dunbar and Berwick. Berwick retains as many as 17 stopping trains a day each way, and Dunbar 10 going south and six going north.

Neither Berwick and Tweedmouth nor Dunbar has any freight, though there are a possible seven or eight trains a day each way passing through. But there have been two remarkable new entrants to local freight trade. A small, historic limestone quarry and mine with a siding at Oxwellmains, south of Dunbar, was expanded from the 1960s by Blue Circle Cement into a vast, two-mile long, opencast operation with smoking cement works, on both sides of the railway, and involving the rerouting of the A1 and the restoration of much of the farmland at a lower level. It does make full use of the railway, with train loads or rakes of cement tankers distributed by EWS to several terminals on Scotland's network; and with incoming loads of waste from Edinburgh for infill. The other entrant, entirely new, is at a private siding near Torness Nuclear Power Station, five miles south east of Dunbar, where flasks of spent radioactive material are loaded for rail transit to Sellafield in Cumbria – the only good thing one can say about this unnecessary giant, which blots our scenic coast for over 10 miles.

Finally, what can an occasional visitor say about the role of the railway in the life and work of people in this region? In and around Berwick and Dunbar it certainly seems to be a life-line for many travellers, especially commuters to Edinburgh, as well as visitors and those going to and from London and the South. For those living and working in between, most of whom are likely to be car users, it is hardly relevant. There are also bus services radiating from Berwick into the Borders and along the coast, supported by Borders Council, and a few, less frequent, out from Dunbar. A two-hourly service from Edinburgh by Perryman diverts from the A1 to call at Innerwick, Bilsdean, Co'path, Coldingham and Eyemouth. It takes an hour and five minutes for the slightly longer journey between Dunbar and Berwick – a useful successor to the 'Berwick Local'! The value of the line for freight, exemplified only by the special users at Oxwellmains and Torness, could surely be exploited at Tweedmouth and Dunbar. Is there not a case for reopening one hub station, such as Tweedmouth or Reston, for general goods and passengers?

The environmental benefit of the railway is obvious to anyone staying nearby. Long trains pass quietly and without pollution since electrification and with little visual intrusion along its 26-foot wide corridor, about four times an hour. In contrast, on the 60-foot swathe of its nearby rival, the A1, a continuous stream of cars and HGVs sweeps stridently and obtrusively past, all day and evening long; and its new embankment at Cockburnspath blocks views from the village and diverts the Southern Upland Way.

Where Was Peter Geddes Born?

Walter Stephen

ONE OF MY WEAKNESSES is that I have always been unable to resist a challenge. At the ceremony in early 2004 for the Scottish Awards for Quality in Planning, an Aberdeenshire official and I were discussing Patrick Geddes and the approaching 150th anniversary of his birth. The official said they would like to put a plaque up on his birthplace. Did I know where it was? I should have known that there would be good reasons for this simple little fact being unknown and that many clever people before us had tried and failed; but airily I said I would do a little research and get back to him well before 2 October.

This modest essay is a record of my rather lengthy quest. At times I thought the quest was a failure; I did not see how we could ever know precisely where Geddes was born. I was forced to take comfort from the belief that on every quest there are interesting diversions and serendipitous discoveries. But PLATE 5A almost shows where Geddes was born – and the facts support me! This essay is not a major contribution to knowledge – it could be said to be a case-study in how not to research a question – but the process of finding the truth has shed a little more illumination on the background and formation of this multi-faceted genius.

Geddes's origins, early life and upbringing are well enough documented, not least by Geddes himself who, in his six *Talks from My/The Outlook Tower* (Survey, 1925), particularly *The Education of Two Boys*, gives much detail of his life at home – after the family had moved to Mount Tabor on Kinnoull Hill, across the Tay from Perth (PLATE 5B).

A start can be made with the registration of his birth, which occurred on 2 October 1854, in the Register of Births of the Parish of Glenmuick, Tullich and Glengairn for 1854. The record says: 'Alexander Geddes, Ballater and his wife Janet Stevenson had a son born.' It repeats that they were married and that the son was baptised Peter. Here we have a double difficulty; Patrick Geddes did not start life as Patrick, but as Peter, and there is no address for the Geddes family.

We are familiar with the birth certificate of today, which has a standard form and gives quite a lot of information about the parents, including the actual address of the birthplace. Annoyingly, it was only in 1855 that compulsory registration of births, with a standard format, was introduced. An oblique approach would thus be necessary to find the birthplace.

We can dispose quickly of the change of name; the place of birth is a little more difficult.

There is nothing terribly significant about Geddes's change of name. Scots have traditionally had a relaxed attitude towards names – in Scotland one can change one's name without Deed Poll. As in the old North-East folk song:

Oh he's titled Glenlogie
Fan he is at hame
He's of the noble Gordons
Lord John is his name.

In fisher towns the small number of family names and the restricted number of Christian names in use produced a rich collection of 'tee-names' – used to differentiate between those with similar names. These could embody a relationship ('Willie's Tam's Jock'), a physical characteristic ('Lugs') or interesting social behaviour (like 'Pan Drops', who had a slight stammer and whose chat-up line at a kirk soiree was 'W-w-w-wid ye like a pan drop?'). Farmers were almost always known by the names of their farms. It took me over 20 years to learn that 'Cunnie', of Conglass ('Cunnie's') had the same surname as myself. While searching the census for this project I discovered that the ferry-man over the Dee at Boat of Dinnet had that same surname – unusual in a place almost 40 miles from the sea. On apprising the local historian of my interesting discovery she said, 'Oh aye, that wid be 'Boatie' Stephen.'

Patrick's mother herself, Janet Geddes, is so named on the register of births (1854) and on her death certificate (1898). But on the census enumerator's Schedule for Perth for 1861, presumably following a less formal procedure – she is recorded as Jessie.

John McKail Geddes, 11 years Patrick's senior, emigrated to New

Zealand in 1862 and regularly wrote home. His descendant, Alex Geddes, also has a collection of letters written from Mount Tabor 1860–88. At first, the letters home conclude by passing on good wishes to Peter, but one addressed to 'My Dear Old Fellow' on 16 February 1863, concludes 'Dear Pat, your brother Johnny'. Then it is back to Peter for a period. By 1864 we have 'My Dear Pat', 'Love to Pat', 'My Dear Wee Pat', 'Pat is a very clever little fellow'. Letters from his mother and sister refer consistently to 'Pat' and 'Patie'.

That the change of name was a teenage conceit of the son, rather than an imposition by a doting family, is suggested by two of the young Patrick's letters to John (Jack). One, written about 1865, is signed 'Peter', the other, written in 1870, is signed 'Pat'. Perhaps, for Geddes, 'Peter' personified authority and orthodoxy, while Patrick, often shown expounding the Trinity by referring to the humble shamrock, was more the kind of model he aspired to.

For the birthplace, the family letters might also seem the best starting point. However, Alex Geddes from New Zealand regrets:

> to say that there is nothing here to indicate where Patrick was born; none of the letters indicate the address of the house in Ballater and we have no envelopes. Aunt Mary (Patrick's niece) inherited letters written home to Scotland by her father John McKail and a few very early letters prior to his emigration, she mentioned once that her brother Bob had inherited the majority of the replies to the letters but burnt them with the words 'Nobody will ever want to read these'.

So much for family pride!

The Census of Scotland, taken every 10 years since 1801 (except, for obvious reasons, in 1941) records every individual present in every household on census night (usually in Spring). The 1851 census might show the Geddes family in residence in Ballater. In fact, there was no person by the name of Geddes in Ballater, in the parish (Glenmuick, Tullich and Glengairn) or in the next parish (Crathie – of interest as the parish in which Balmoral Castle is situated). However, even if there had been a Geddes family, at that date Ballater, although planned, was still a village with four rudimentary streets, no street names nor any house names. From 1861 the census showed for every house the number of windowed rooms it had (from which it might have been possible to sort out one surviving house from another) but in 1851 this could not be done. There seemed little point in trudging around the Ballater of today, clipboard in hand, plotting those houses definitely dating from the 1850s.

By 1861 the family had moved to Perth, to Mount Tabor, a villa suburb on the wooded slopes of Kinnoull Hill. I am not aware that any writer has commented on the name of their house – Mount Tabor Cottage. Mount Tabor (*Jebel et Tur* – Mountain of Mountains – as the Arabs call it) is distinguished among the mountains of Palestine for its picturesque site, its graceful outline, and for the remarkable vegetation which covers its rocky, calcareous, side. There is a splendid view from its summit, which is traditionally the scene of Christ's Transfiguration. In a household such as the Geddes's this would be well known and, if one's early environment has any influence at all on adult thinking, the young Patrick would already be seeing Kinnoull Hill and the Sidlaws as more than crags and volcanic sills, covered in fine woodland and follies aping Rhenish castles admired on the Grand Tour.

The household was made up as follows:

Alexander Geddes	Head	52	Quarter Master Perthshire Militia Chelsea Pensioner	(born) Invernessshire, Inverallan
Jessie Geddes	Wife	44		Lanarkshire, Airdrie
Robert Geddes	Son	22	Bank Clerk	Ireland
Jessie Geddes	Daughter	19		Angus, Forfar
John Geddes	Son	17	Lawyer's Clerk Apprentice	Malta
Peter Geddes	Son	6	Scholar	Ballater Aberdeenshire,
Lenore(?) B. Fisher	Servant	25	Domestic Servant	Perthshire, Scone

In the wake of the repeal of the Window Tax and the concern for clean air and healthy sunlight, the census enumerator noted that the Geddes ménage had six rooms with one or more windows. But, if we accept one person per room as acceptable, there was a degree of over-crowding – soon to be relieved as the two elder brothers moved off to seek their fortunes, leaving Patrick to be brought up by his ageing parents and an older sister whose fiancé died at 24 and who did not marry.

The family were well enough off to keep a servant, no miserable ragged tweenie, but a mature lass from the next parish.

Father was a senior non-commissioned officer who had three times refused the offer of a commission and was then commissioned in the militia. Long and distinguished service had been recognised by the award of a pension and by his continuing employment with the local militia. That his duties were not too onerous can be assumed from the fact that the Victoria Street Soldiers' Barracks held little more than a handful of ageing NCOs and their wives from the 42nd (Black Watch) and 92nd (Gordons). There would be time to cultivate his garden and teach the young Patrick how, for example, to plant potatoes or make a box.

Where the children were born is an interesting comment on the military life. As the regiment was moved around the world, the wives followed. Hence Ireland, Malta and, I think, Ballater. With Jessie's birth in Forfar it is likely that mother had been sent 'home' for health reasons, the regiment having transferred from the Ionian Islands to Malta in 1842. We know that Patrick's mother worked as a teacher for the military families when on foreign service.

Elsewhere (in 'Patrick Geddes – the Life' in *Think Global, Act Local: The Life and Legacy of Patrick Geddes*) I have commented on the equivocal status of the Army officer promoted from the ranks. On paper Alexander's life was a success, from nothing to (to quote his death certificate) 'Captain 42nd Royal Highlanders'. But how did he fit in with his neighbours? Who were his neighbours?

In this developing leafy suburb of Perth, ancient market and county town, major railway and textile centre, Geddes's neighbouring house-holders – in big houses with many servants – included:

Shipping Emigration Agent	Bank Secretary
Banker (Secretary to Central Bank of Scotland)	Editor (*Perthshire Advertiser*)
Upholsterer (employer of 27 men, 10 boys and 5 women)	Landed Proprietor
Superintendent of Lunatic Asylum	'Kept by Family'

(A quantitative measure of the social gap between the Geddes family and the eight neighbouring households comes from the 1861 Census. Average rooms per household – 10.6 [Mount Tabor Cottage – 6]. Residents per household – 5.5 [Mount Tabor – 7]. Resident servants – 1.1 [Mount Tabor – 1].)

Patrick himself described the close family life inside the garden walls and the laboratory/workshop built by his father for his year of 'home studies'. There were rambles over Kinnoull Hill with his father and alone, and longer expeditions over the Grampians. To be fair, he also describes ploys and mischief with his schoolfellows, but the overall impression is of a tight-knit family slightly out of place. I am not suggesting that the neighbours consciously considered the Geddes family 'not one of us' – indeed, Alexander may not have wished to move 'beyond his station' – but it is likely that there was, quite simply, little in common between the globetrotters in the cottage and the local bourgeoisie in the big houses.

Ballater is a small place but it is in no way ordinary. It is on Royal Deeside. It is the nearest town to Balmoral and has a formidable collection of Royal Warrant holders – 'By Appointment'. From 1866 it was the railhead of the Deeside Railway, whose westward extension was blocked by no less a personage than HM Queen Victoria. Some will be familiar with old film showing a kilted guard of honour at Ballater Station being inspected by the reigning monarch; the guard probably being a detachment of the Gordon Highlanders, brought out from Aberdeen.

The royal presence on Deeside dates from 8 September 1848, when Victoria and Albert stayed at the old Balmoral Castle for the first time. They went to the Highlands for privacy – and they found it. On that first visit there were no soldiers and only one policeman. The Balmoral estate was leased for 38 years from 1836, and in 1852 it was bought by

Prince Albert. On 28 September 1853, the Queen laid the foundation stone of the new Balmoral Castle and on 7 September 1855 she stayed in the new castle for the first time.

In those early days it was the practice for the Queen to travel north by Royal Train to Perth, spend the night there and, next morning, proceed by coach through Blairgowrie and Braemar to Deeside. Perth was the depot of the 42nd Foot, the Royal Highlanders, the Black Watch, the senior Highland regiment, and there was a logic to the Black Watch being responsible for royal duties. While the new Balmoral was building there was probably a need for some show of authority in the area. Who better to command a small detachment than a senior, sober but underemployed ex-sergeant major from the Volunteers, the Black Watch being otherwise engaged at the Alma in the Crimea 12 days before Patrick was born?

The above seemed the most likely explanation of why Peter/ Patrick Geddes was born in Ballater. Did Janet Geddes lodge in Ballater while her husband commuted daily to Balmoral? Or did he camp on site during the week and come back to Ballater at the weekends?

Another possibility required to be examined. In the correspondence between John and Mount Tabor it became clear that Alexander Geddes had a brother on Deeside who was ill in the early part of 1864. On 17 August, John wrote from Auckland on 'The sad news of Uncle's death... Poor Aunt... left with such a large family'. In September, Alexander was in Braemar at trustees' meetings, no doubt tidying up the affairs of his late brother, John.

From Dunedin on 10 November 1864, John Geddes wrote to Jessie, his sister, as follows:

> Your jaunt up to the highlands must have been very pleasant the village of Ballater must have improved very much it is almost a pity Father sold his property there, but more pleasant still would it be to meet your Old school companions

confirming a fairly permanent presence in the village, lasting beyond Alexander's actual employment in the area. It looked as if Alexander had inherited his brother's house and sold it almost immediately.

Working on the hypothesis that Patrick Geddes's family lodged with brother John when they were in the Balmoral area, and using the approximate dates from the letters, details of John's house might be found from the General Register of Sasines, in which all transfers of feudal property are recorded. Unfortunately, no record of any Geddes-related sale of property was to be found for 1864–65. Only one Geddes appears in the Aberdeenshire index around that time, and he was an Aberdeen merchant. No will for a John Geddes in Aberdeenshire can be traced, either.

Once again the quest seemed to be up against a granite wall. But, remembering the Duke of Wellington's dictum – 'Push on until you are stopped, then go round' – another approach was tried, this time with success. The valuation roll for Aberdeenshire, parish of Glenmuick, lists all properties valued at £4 or over for the year 1856. For example, William Sherriffs, Surgeon, Ballater owned a house of yearly value £18 and had living next door 'sundry occupiers under £4 year', their little houses totalling £19. Were the Geddes family unable to afford a house of £4 value? And therefore did not show up in the record?

Folio 6 gave the answer. On line 12 it is recorded that 'Alex Geddes, Ensign & Alex Geddes, Ballater' had a 'House and Feu ground'. The house was occupied by Eliza Farquharson, Ballater while the entry on line 13 was occupied by William Troup, Flesher. In Scotland, a flesher was one who sold meat, while the butcher killed the animals. This is important to remember when we come to examine PLATE 5A and seek to determine how it was used. The rents were respectively £12.50 for the house and £8 for the butcher's shop. In the valuation roll these names have been ruled out and another hand has written in 'now William Ross' for lines 12 and 13. Now we have real evidence that the Geddes family owned a decent house in Ballater, indeed a more than decent property, since it included a shop whose value made the combined property worth more than the surgeon's house. (For purposes of comparison it is interesting to note that, when the family moved to Mount Tabor Cottage (PLATE 5B; the real formative influence on PG) the house of six rooms and garden belonged to David Robertson, Stationer, High Street, Perth and was of yearly rent or value £16.75 – about a quarter more than the Ballater house, suggesting that it probably had only four rooms.)

Where was the Ballater house? Unfortunately, the entries for the village of Ballater are arranged in alphabetical order. All we can say from the roll is that, at that date, there were about 48 decent houses in the village – most of them without shops attached. Fortunately, the Register of Sasines, in its summary and in the full entry for the Geddes house, clearly sets out the location of the property and records the transactions which affected it. Stripped of the legal verbiage, the property was sold to Alexander Geddes and Mrs Janet Stevenson or Geddes, his spouse, on 21 August 1852. Alexander Geddes was late Sergeant, 42nd Regiment of Foot, and was then residing in Ballater. Three children – Robert, Janet and John McKail Geddes – were named in the 1857 disposition. No Patrick, but there can be no doubt that he was born two years after the family moved into the house.

Who sold them the house? None other than William Sherriffs, Surgeon. The Geddes plot was half a feu, with a frontage of 80 feet and a depth of 160, with 'the Dwelling House, Shop and other Erections thereon'. From the boundaries recorded it is possible to identify exactly the plot, those buildings on it which are original and those which are replacements or of post-Geddes construction. Ballater was a planned settlement and some of the pioneer flavour is caught by the entry which records that Geddes bought the plot and house 'together with the right of taking stones for the purposes of building on the said piece from the North Craig of Ballater, the said stones being always carried by the common county road'.

The back lane of the 1857 record has become Albert Road, but it is still possible to look around and discern the outlines of the original feu, with its fine granite boundary wall and the house and shop on the north side, facing the Square, and the north-east corner. As Ballater grew in size and prosperity the east side of the feu was built up in some style, with two substantial 1½-storey villas, now containing the premises of two Royal Warrant holders. In 1906 the corner site was completely rebuilt in keeping with its strategic location in the now prepossessing little town. In the best of beautiful granite, a two-storey block of shops below and flats above dominates the corner, proudly displaying the date of building and quite outshining the earlier house next door. I was satisfied that, on this modestly substantial two-storey house (PLATE 5A), there could now be attached something of this sort:

In this house, on 2 October 1854, was born
Patrick (Peter) Geddes (1854–1932)
Biologist
Town Planner
Re-educator
Peace-warrior

'Think Global, Act Local'
'By Leaves We Live'

and that the happy occasion could be marked with a procession led by a piper, Geddes-style.

On reflection, however, as I studied the premises now occupied by Rowan Antiques, I felt there was something not quite right. The arrangement of doors and windows, virtually unaltered since 1857, does not conform to the local style of central front door with two flanking windows on the ground floor and three windows on the first floor. Reluctantly, I have to accept that this was not the Geddes birth-house, but the shop, with flat above, let out to William Troup the flesher. 'Modified rapture,' as Nanki-poo says in *The Mikado*.

The Geddes birthhouse must have been swept away by the property developer in 1906. The end of the handsome new block (new a century ago!) can be seen on the left of PLATE 5A. The wording on the plaque will be required to be less forceful now.

What happened to the house? On 26 November 1857, Alexander Geddes, now Quartermaster, Royal Perthshire Rifles, and residing at Mount Tabor, near Perth, sold it to 'William Ferguson, House Carpenter, formerly residing at San Francisco, now at Newton of Gairn' (just north of Ballater). Is there the beginnings of another quest here? Was Ferguson one of the lucky ones who made it in the California Gold Rush and came back home to flaunt his hard-won wealth? Did this influence young John McKail, who emigrated to New Zealand and caught 'gold fever' there? In 1863 he wrote apologetically to his father, ashamed to mention it but too honest to conceal it. But the lad was only 19! The Geddes children were 18, 15, 13 and 2 when the Ballater house was sold, all but Patrick well able to have made friends and to have accumulated memories from their time there.

Personally it is satisfying to have come to the end of the quest, but – does it matter? Is this not just mere antiquarianism? Is Charlie the goose alive and well and strutting across the Square at Ballater? I would suggest not, but that the location of Geddes's place and style of birth, reinforced by the study of his father's service record, which follows, is important for our understanding of Geddes and his works.

Patrick Geddes is often cited as the archetypical 'lad o'pairts' of Scots tradition, but this is an over-simplification. Think of Mary Symon's great poem of the First World War – 'The Glen's Muster Roll: The Dominie Loquitor':

… You – Robbie. Memory pictures; Front bench, a curly pow.
A chappit hannie grippin' ticht a *Homer* men't wi' tow –
The lave a' scrammelin' near him, like bummies roon a bike.
'Fat's this?' 'Fat's that?' he'd tell them a' – ay, speir they fat they
    like.
My hill-foot lad! A sowl and brain fae's bonnet to his beets,
A 'Fullerton' in posse, nae the first fun' fowin' peats.

(A 'Fullarton': winner of the Fullarton Scholarship at Aberdeen University – Editor)

In later life, Geddes preached an education of Head, Heart and Hand. With his father he learnt how to plant potatoes. He was a gardener, by precept and example. As an old man he enjoyed working with his hands among the stones of the growing Scots College – yet there is no record of his ever having to endure the grinding effects of poverty and hard physical labour, such as loading peats. The young Geddes never went barefoot to school. And he grew up in a household with a live-in servant.

When searching the valuation rolls I had found myself questioning whether a man of the calibre of Alexander Geddes could possibly end up as a 'sundry occupier of under £4 per year'. At some length, in *Think Global, Act Local* and above, and in Geddes's own *The Education of Two Boys*, it has been made clear that there was a duality in the Geddes home and upbringing. On the one hand, the home was secure and loving, with parents who spent time with their son and who were amazingly tolerant of his behaviour – unconventional for the time and place. On the other hand, it was quite a modest home and the Geddes parents were little people with no great weight in society. Still the Ballater birthplace was not a miserable hovel; it was quite a substantial investment – and there was a shop, too.

The two older boys rose in the conventional manner, by industry and integrity – and by emigrating. (Robert married a general's daughter and John became a successful merchant in New Zealand, dealing in coffee and spices.) Mac Geddes, John's youngest son, said, in 1937:

> My own father... as an unshaven lad of seventeen years, came all the way from Scotland, alone and because of his own self reliance made an honourable name for himself and complete independence before he was thirty.

But Patrick chose a difficult path, working in the bank for a time then leaving for a period of 'home studies'; attending Edinburgh University for a week before rejecting what it had to offer. Somehow he had acquired the self-confidence – this amorphously qualified provincial – to study under T.H. Huxley, to disagree with him and yet be helped to advancement by him. Geddes never made a fortune (quite the opposite) but throughout his life contrived to find a series of patrons for his schemes. All his life he mixed, on equal terms, with some of the best thinkers in three continents. Never a member of the establishment, he was on good terms with two viceroys and was twice offered a knighthood (but never under a Conservative regime). His entry in *Who's Who 1930* amounted to 334 words – not bad for the son of an obscure soldier from a little Perthshire cottage.

Geddes was an admirable person in so many respects. Not least he evokes admiration for the way in which, in his life, he carried with him the positive aspects of his birth and upbringing while, apparently, oblivious to what jealous rivals might have used against him.

PLATE I

The Geddes Panels

From top to bottom, *Flos Herbae,* Lilies, Valley Section.

(Patrick Geddes Memorial Trust)

PLATE 2A

Helen Williamson, Senior Library Officer, Department of Art and Music, Edinburgh Central Library, examines the Geddes model.

(Patrick Geddes Memorial Trust)

PLATE 2B

Sonar Tari – Golden Boat, Kolkata, April 2004

(Kenny Munro)

PLATE 3A

Sonar Tari – Bengal Boat, Ballater, October 2004

(Kenny Munro)

PLATE 3B

Dunglass Dean – four fine bridges
Taken from 1798 bridge, railway viaduct, post-war A1 concrete bridge, 1930s
A1 concrete arched bridge.

(Frank Spaven)

PLATE 4A
Royal Border Bridge, 1964
Now in its third century of service.
(Frank Spaven)

PLATE 4B

Penmanshiel,
8 March 1979
Two days before the
tunnel collapsed, two
men died – perhaps
among those in the
photograph.
(Frank Spaven)

PLATE 5A

Was Peter/Patrick Geddes born here?

(Walter Stephen)

PLATE 5B

Mount Tabor Cottage, Perth
The Geddes family home.

(Kenneth MacLean)

Former course of Cowie
Water

(Walter Stephen)

Stonehaven and the site of the marine station from the south
(Andy Gray)

Detail from the Valley Section
The Fisher lives and works where the Cowie Water enters the sea.
(Patrick Geddes Memorial Trust)

PLATE 7

Walpurgis Strasse, Dresden, March 2006

Nothing survives of the former No 21, but the civilised atmosphere of the old street has been successfully transmitted to the new.

(Sophia Leonard)

PLATE 8A
Festspielhaus, Hellerau, 2003
(Walter Stephen)

PLATE 8B
Area basement in
St Andrew Square,
Edinburgh, 2006
(Walter Stephen)

Appendix
Alexander Geddes's Service and Pension Records

Biographers of Geddes – and Geddes himself – have emphasised the importance of the home and local environment in his development. His father receives special attention, while he is generally given more than a mention, his background has not been fully described, or has been slightly romanticised. His service and pension records have not been quoted before and are now summarised below as a contribution to knowledge and as a complement to the essay above. The justification for this Appendix is that it provides hard evidence for some of the general statements made about the Geddes family and particularly for their equivocal social position in Perth's 'leafy suburb' on the lower slopes of Kinnoull Hill.

Inevitably there is a good deal of repetition (e.g. date and place of birth) in this material. In the interests of clarity and brevity the non-specific, printed material in the records has been kept to a minimum and some information is quoted in one place only.

Editorial comment is expressed in *italics*.

Sources – British Army Records

Service Records – WO 97/577/100 (42nd Foot)

Out-Pensions of Royal Hospital, Chelsea, 1715–1913 – WO 116/59 (Cavalry and Infantry, 1851)

Records of Officers' Services, 1764–1961 – WO 76/420 (Perthshire Militia)

Royal Hospital, Chelsea, Discharge Documents of Pensioners 1760–1887 – WO 121 – nil

Royal Hospital, Chelsea, Documents of Soldiers Awarded Deferred Pensions 1838–1896 – WO 131 – nil

Record of Service in 42nd Foot (Black Watch)

Attestation for Unlimited Service – dated Paisley, 25 December 1826, states that Alexander Geddes, Labourer, born in Inverallen Parish, Inverness-shire, enlisted himself on 23 December, was found fit for service and received a Bounty of two pounds, two shillings.

(2 guineas, or £2.10 – 'the King's shilling'. Grantown-on-Spey is the largest settlement in the parish of Inverallen. If the Death Certificate is correct in recording AG's father as 'Merchant (deceased)' he was probably a shopkeeper in Grantown.)

Alexander appeared to be 15 years old, 5 feet 3 inches high, fresh complexion, brown eyes, brown hair.

(AG in the pension records is recorded as born on 28/11/1810. Boardman, Kitchen etc. give 1808 as his year of birth.)

Record of Service	23/12/1826 – 22/12/1829	Drummer	(Under Age)
	(Not pensionable service.)		
	23/12/1829 – 19/6/1831	Drummer	1 Year 189 days
	20/6/1831 – 30/6/1831	Tried for absenting himself without leave. Guilty for which imprisoned.	

(This sentence did not count as pensionable service. An uncomfortable fact – why did AG go 'on the trot'? Homesickness? Bullying? A romantic entanglement?)

1/7/1831 – 31/12/1832	Drummer	1 Year 184 days	
1/1/1833 – 12/8/1834	Private	1 Year 224 days	
13/8/1834 – 31/3/1836	Corporal	1 Year 232 days	
1/4/1836 – 31/3/1843	Serjeant	7 Years	
Service abroad –	Corfu	2 Years 298 days	
	Malta	4 Years 31 days	
	Bermuda	4 Years 101 days	

(Alexander's service abroad was that of peacetime garrison duty.)
(The Ionian Islands were subject to Venice from 1386 to 1797. From 1814 to 1864 they were a republic dependent on Great Britain – hence the presence of the 42nd. In 1862 the new king of Greece, a Danish prince who ruled as George I, requested that Britain give up their 'protectorate' of the Ionian Islands as a condition of his accession to the Greek throne and in 1863 the islanders voted to transfer to Greece. A form of cricket is still played there.)

1/4/1843 – 31/3/1850	Serjeant Major	7 Years
1/4/1850 – 22/10/1851	Serjeant	1 Year 205 days 'On reduction of the establishment'

(In other words, administrative necessity – no blame attached to AG.)

Total – 21 Years 304 days

(Robert Geddes was born in Ireland – which was not service abroad in 1839. The regiment was at Limerick that year. Jessie was born at Forfar in 1842, when her father was serving in Corfu and Malta. John was born in Malta in 1844.)

Proposed Discharge – Aberdeen Barracks, 22/10/1851 – Acting Serjeant Major Alexander Geddes – 'having been found unfit for further service, as per Medical Officer's Certificate attached.'

Character and Conduct – 'his general character has been very good, having been a non-commissioned officer for upwards of 17 years – 7 years of which he was Serjt Major in the Brown Bn. He has been once tried by Regtl Court Martial on 21 June 1831 for absence without leave but does not appear in any Defaulter Book but for that offence.'

(The Army may forgive, but it never forgets.)

'Intended place of Residence – Airdrie, Lanarkshire.'

(Interesting, it looks as if the family were proposing to settle with or near Mrs Geddes's family. They had not been in Perth for many years.)

Medical Report – The nature of this man's Disability is **General Debility & Emaciation** the result of long military service & Climate – has neither been induced nor encreased *(sic)* by intemperance or other vice. In a word, he is '**worn out**' – Is recommended for Discharge.

Opinion of Principal Medical Officer, Chatham, 5/11/1851 – After examination I am of opinion that Serjt Major Alexr Geddes is unfit for Senior work, likely to be permanently disqualified.

Horse Guards 25/11/1851 – The Discharge of the Man above mentioned is approved by the General Commander-in-Chief.

Description, Chatham, 25/11/1851 – as above, save for age – 40 Years *(his 41st birthday was on 20/11/1851)* – and height, now 5 Feet 9¼ inches.

(1851 was probably a good time to retire Geddes. In that year the Black Watch ended its Bermuda tour of duty and was posted to Halifax, Nova Scotia. Directly or via Britain? I cannot say. In 1852 they were back in Stirling, Perth and Dundee.)

Alexander Geddes, Chelsea Pensioner

Examination of Invalid Soldiers – 42nd Foot – Colour Serjt/Acting Serjt Major Alexander Geddes – Character Very Fine – Awarded Pension of 2/6 per week.

(= 12.5p per week. Of twelve entries on the page, this is the most generous. Below Geddes is Serjt Alexander Wright, also of the 42nd. Both he and Geddes were awarded 2/ – 10p – but another hand has changed the award to Geddes and has justified it by minuscule reference to a letter to the War Office on 1/7/1857. The same hand also awards him three additional years of service. Alexander must have had at least one friend in a high place.)

Service in the Perthshire Militia

Service and Dates of Commission

Ensign or Cornet	23 February 1855 (Date of Full Pay)
Lieutenant	5 November 1855
Quartermaster	22 November 1856
Quartermaster	25 February 1874 (57 Brigade Depot)

Total Commissioned Service

to 31/3/1878	23 Years and 37 days
Total Service in the Ranks	21 Years and 338 days

(In the record the printed rank 'Captain' is scored out and 'Quartermaster' substituted twice. Clearly the Army never considered AG to be a captain, which was probably a courtesy title given locally to save lengthy explanations. On his death certificate AG is 'Captain 42nd Royal Highlanders', which is clearly inaccurate but understandable.)

(Where was Peter Geddes born? How do the records help? They add to our frustration. We have four fixed points, with irritating gaps between.

But the Register of Sasines helps with (a) and (b) below

1 *On 25/11/1851 AG was discharged at Chatham with the intention of settling in Airdrie*

a *On 21/8/1852 AG bought house in Ballater.*

2 *On 2/10/1854 Peter/Patrick was born in Ballater*

3 *On 23/2/1855 AG was commissioned as Cornet or Ensign at Perth*

4 *On 1/7/1857 AG was credited with 3 additional years of service, which do not appear on his Service Record or his Perthshire Militia record.*

b *26/11/1857 AG sold house in Ballater.*

Without detailed records for the Perthshire Militia we cannot be sure, but the sequence of events may have been something like this: On discharge, Geddes had no clear idea – at 41 – as to his next move. As a reliable and senior former non-commissioned officer he was taken on for the militia for the Balmoral responsibility – although the three years and additional 6d per week pension were added to his 42nd Foot total. We know that he had earlier declined a regular commission but one in the militia must have been more congenial.

After three years the family moved to Perth permanently. Alexander would be competent, was promoted but probably not overtaxed, leaving ample scope for family life, and especially for the burgeoning talents of his gifted son.)

The Light Before the Darkness

Anne-Michelle Slater

The Scottish Zoological Station, Cowie

THE INAUGURATION OF the Scottish Zoological Station at Cowie took place on Thursday 7 August 1879. The *Stonehaven Journal* stated that the station was situated close to the seashore on the north side of the village of Cowie and immediately in front of a little creek. The opening ceremony was conducted by Mr G.J. Romanes, FRS, London, in the presence of Professor and Mrs James Cossar Ewart, Professor of Natural History at the University of Aberdeen; Mrs Principal Pirie and Miss Pirie, and others, including Major Innes of Raemoir and Cowie.

Reports of the day indicate that the proceedings started with 'luncheon spread out on the sea beach'. The guest list seems to indicate that it was very much an outing for the ladies and one can picture the beautiful white Victorian summer dresses, parasols and large hats. Whether Patrick Geddes was there or not, it is clear from the opening speech, made by Mr Romanes, that this was a very significant moment in the establishment of scientific research facilities in Britain. He was reported as follows:

> ... that it might appear a curious fact that although they in Great Britain pride themselves on being the ruler of the waves, they nevertheless displayed so little curiosity in ascertaining what those waves have to teach us about their inhabitants. When they looked upon that building they must feel that it is a remarkable thing that it is the only building of its kind in Great Britain, for although there are several zoological stations, large and well equipped in several parts of Europe, this is the first that has been reared in this country. They must consider it a credit to Aberdeen University that it should have taken the initiative in founding such an institution... [and] the fact will always remain in history that Aberdeen University was the first to found an institution of this kind.

Professor Cossar Ewart proposed a vote of thanks and Mrs Pirie, the Principal's wife, conducted what was referred to as a christening of the larger of the two boats to be used by the zoological station. It was named the *Aphrodite* and was then used for the company to sail 'some distance to sea'. There was no mention of Patrick Geddes. At that time he was a 25 year old demonstrator and not worthy of mention in the newspaper. Perhaps while lunch was being served, Geddes was inside eagerly looking at the first specimens or making sure that all was in place for the party's inspection. His impetuous nature, however, may have meant that, as his work was primarily in setting up the research station, he had taken the opportunity to absent himself, on the occasion of the formal opening, to further his plans for a trip to Mexico, in a month's time.

Background

My own knowledge and understanding of Geddes began when I came across this name, by staying for a week at the Patrick Geddes Halls of Residence during the Edinburgh Festival in 1979. Not the original ones in Ramsay Garden, but recently refurbished accommodation, named in recognition of the man who had first established self-governing students' residences in Great Britain: student halls, providing an alternative to living in college or in lodgings. During that time, I also visited the Outlook Tower and the Camera Obscura, but cannot recollect if the connection with the man after whom my accommodation was named was apparent. If it had been, then no doubt I wondered at the diversity of this individual, as Philip Boardman states:

> those who hear about him for the first time, quite understand-
> ably, regard him as a disperse jack of all trades, shuttling
> among jumbles of now academic, now practical interest.

I next came across the name as a postgraduate Planning student at University College, Dublin, where Professor Michael Bannon taught Planning History, linking Geddes with Lord and Lady Aberdeen, Viceroy and Vicereine in 1911. Lady Aberdeen, in particular, was deeply involved in the problems of the Irish poor and in their joint reminiscences.

She wrote:

> We endeavoured to stir up public feeling on this subject [Irish urban deprivation] and with this end in view invited Professor Geddes to bring his City and Town Planning Exhibition to Dublin, guaranteeing him against loss. He came, not once, but twice, and he and the Exhibition made a deep impression on a small circle of earnest students (see FIG 11).

The reminiscences were titled *We Twa* – an allusion to Burns:

> We twa hae run aboot the braes,
> And pu'd the gowans fine...

> We twa hae paidled in the burn,
> Frae morning sun till dine...

> For auld lang syne...

Two direct consequences of Geddes's visits to Dublin were a campaign to clean up some of the estimated 2,000 derelict sites in the city and turn several into children's playgrounds, and the establishment of the Housing and Town Planning Association in Ireland.

At Heriot-Watt, in the Scottish Planning History classes, I was for the first time really made aware of the breadth and depth of Geddes's influence. At that time, I was more particularly impressed by Charles Rennie Mackintosh and the linkages between traditional Scottish architecture and modernism, but the Geddes link between planning, architecture and social change also permeated my thinking – as it did for all the students of that period, who often felt themselves at odds with the height of Thatcherism and her demotion of the post-war planning principles. Via planning in London, East Anglia and Kincardineshire, by 1999 I was teaching Planning and Law at the Department of Land Economy, University of Aberdeen. I introduced Marine Resource Management undergraduates to law and in so doing, I became interested in the emerging concept of marine spatial planning: a planning system for the sea. Following University reorganisation, I moved to the Law School and started to research and publish on marine spatial planning.

I gave a presentation on planning and marine issues at the Scottish Planning and Environmental Law conference in 2003. The reception that I received clarified for me that the concept of a planning system for the sea and the links between the terrestrial and the marine planning systems would be very hard for mainstream land use planning practitioners to comprehend, particularly at a time of increasing pressures and change in the Scottish planning system. Luckily, I then read an article about Patrick Geddes by Mindy Grewar (of the Ballater Geddes Group), in which she refers to his involvement with a marine research station at Stonehaven. This was a eureka moment! As the link between land and marine planning, the father of town planning worked on my local coastline. I resolved to find out more. The resulting work forms the basis of this essay.

Marine Research in 1879

Why would a marine research station have been considered so important in 1879? In the mid-Victorian era, the deep oceans were almost as mysterious as outer space – remote and offering only a few tantalising clues as to what might be found by the first explorers. Early Victorian debates about the age of the earth and natural selection drew much of their evidence from the exposed rocks of the local coastline and the marine creatures which lived amongst them as memories of the recent Napoleonic Wars had left most scientists afraid to explore deeper waters. When the seas around Great Britain became safer, as the century progressed, scientific interest extended to the high seas. In 1872, the government commissioned a three-year scientific study of the oceans, which produced the greatest additions ever made to biological knowledge by a single expedition: HMS *Challenger*. The study of marine life was therefore of the highest priority and interest in the academic world in the period after 1872. Why, however, was the first marine sation located at Cowie, of all places?

Cowie

About 500 million years ago, the region to the north of what is now Stonehaven began to undergo compression and elevation. A violent burst of volcanic activity formed what has become known as the Highland Boundary Fault, which runs from Garron Point, north of Cowie, diagonally through Scotland to Helensburgh. To the north of this line are hard Dalradian rocks, to the south, a reddish sandstone – the Old Red Sandstone. Any point along the fault is therefore an excellent location for field geology and palaeontology. For example, in 2004, a fossil of the world's oldest air breathing creature was discovered at Cowie. Even in Victorian times, this area would have been recognised as rich in natural history and a particularly suitable location for marine research.

FIG 7 shows how in 1902, at Stonehaven, two small rivers joined just before they entered the sea. The more northerly, the Cowie Water, was interesting and notorious. As Groome's *Ordnance Gazetteer of Scotland, Volume II* (1882) informs us, 'Cowie Water is subject to high freshets, which often do considerable damage.' In 1902, as we can see, the river reached the sea by flowing behind a long shingle spit, but the area was in constant flux – by the 1923 revision the sea (as defined by the high water mark of ordinary spring tides) had advanced by 30 yards and was lapping the base of the bandstand. Not surprisingly, the river has broken through the gravel spit from time to time and now flows directly into the sea through a fortress-like concrete channel – already almost half-blocked by cobbles and shingle (PLATE 6A).

So, an interesting and varied coast, with a guarantee of rich and varied marine pickings.

Cowie itself, as can be seen from the 1902 map, was not much of a place, with no proper harbour – the boats had to be hauled up on the shore when not at sea. In 1845 the 'sea-toun' of Cowie had 174 inhabitants and, supposedly, greater wealth and importance than Stonehaven itself. By the time the marine station arrived, however, its fortunes had declined. Like all small fishing stations it was left behind by the advancing technology of fishhunting, processing and distribution. Many families moved north to Torry, once a royal burgh but in the 19th century developing as a fishing district of Aberdeen, next to

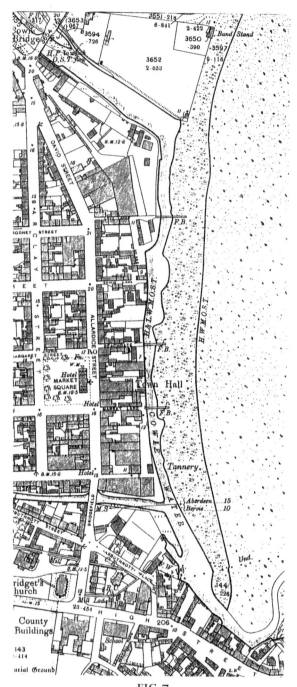

FIG 7

Mouth of Cowie Water, Stonehaven, 1902
(Ordnance Survey, 1/2,500 map)

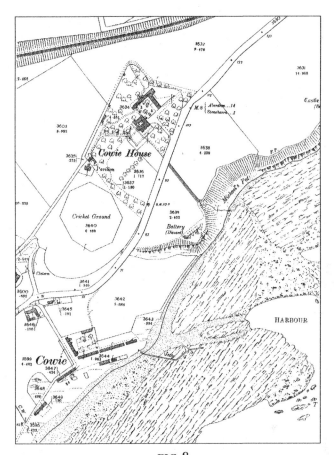

FIG 8
Cowie in 1902
(Ordnance Survey, 1/2,500 map)

the city's expanding harbour. The decline of Cowie was also in part due
to the shipwreck of a Swedish vessel, the *Wihemena Gabb*, on Sunday
11 September 1864, on rocks near the village. The entire crew was res-
cued and taken into the cottages to recover. One of the shipwrecked
sailors, however, was suffering from cholera 'of a violent nature and
of a virulent nature'. It swept through the village and within a few
weeks between 20 and 30 able bodied fishermen and numerous women
and children had died. Cowie never really recovered from this and it
was then the beginning of the end for the local fishing industry. No
doubt the great storm of 14 October 1881, which (literally) decimated

all the East Coast fisher towns, also took a terrible toll. In 1879, however, fishing was still the main occupation of the inhabitants, with a community skilled in the handling of boats and the finding of fish. A self-contained fishing village would have been regarded as an eminently suitable place to locate a marine research station.

The crucial locational factor for the marine station at Cowie, however, was the gift of the drill hall by Major Innes (He also provided one of the station's two boats). Alexander Innes Esquire of Cowie and Raemoir, Major of the Stonehaven Artillery Volunteers, inherited the estate in 1863. He was said to be 'very soldiery' and recruited a number of men from the village, equipping them with belts and swords. He had three gun embrasures constructed on top of the cliff above Cowie (see FIG 8), with a powder magazine nearby. It is interesting to consider why such an enthusiastic gunnery officer should provide his drill hall for the advancement of science, particularly, as the Volunteers were not fully disbanded until 1910. There was no immediate threat of war in the late 1870s and as it appears to have been quite a large building, he must have felt it was time to put it to another use. It has already been noted that developments in natural history at the time had popular appeal and Innes was reported as being eager to assist in whatever way possible. There may also have been a more tangible link with the University, indeed an extensive collection of Innes papers was bequeathed to the University of Aberdeen library special collections when the last Laird of Cowie died in 1975.

Major Innes seems to have been a hard man, rather feared by the villagers. On one occasion, when the Royal Train was passing on its way to Aberdeen and Ballater, with Queen Victoria aboard, he ordered a salute to be fired in her honour. The Queen apparently received such a shock that she ordered that his excessive loyalty be rewarded with a reprimand. No doubt the villagers sniggered behind their hands.

One reason for the current lack of recognition of the marine station is that it was not actually at Cowie for very long – only a few months in fact. Aberdeen University was a very young institution in 1879, the separate King's College in the Old Town and Marischal College in the New having only been amalgamated in 1860. It is not surprising that what turned out to be a small-time venture in a short-term location failed to make an impact in the university records at a time when the university governing body was mainly concerned about the improvement of the buildings at Marischal College – culminating in the supreme achievement in granite as a building material, the famous facade of 1891.

Did Major Innes know that the station would only be located at Cowie for two or three months before it was closed, dismantled and stored in Aberdeen? The following year it was reassembled at the Cromarty Firth; at Oban in 1881; and finally at Hilton on the Moray Firth in 1883. Was it always anticipated that it would be peripatetic, collecting new data every year? The *Stonehaven Journal* had pointed out that:

> the building contained the excellent qualification of being movable from place to place, being built in sections which are bolted together and can very easily and in a short time be taken down.

The newspaper reports also indicated that some students lived at the station when it was at Cowie and used it as a temporary residence. This capacity to house reaserchers would probably have been even more important when it moved away from the relatively local vicinity of Stonehaven, some 15 miles from Aberdeen and the university to which it was connected. It should be noted that two further marine research stations were subsequently established in Scotland; at Granton in 1884 and Millport in 1897. Aberdeen University marine research stations seem to have fallen into disuse around this time, however, as no further references to them have been found after 1883.

Geddes's Role in the Marine Station

The establishment of the marine station was one of the first tasks that Geddes undertook, after ending his time as a student Paddy Kitchen refers to his 'incompliant relationship with the educational establishment in the Scottish capital'. He abandoned Edinburgh University after one week and, as he had been reading Thomas Huxley's lay sermons, formed a 'burning desire' to study under Huxley in London. To do this, he needed his parents' continued financial and moral support, as Huxley was at that time the most outspoken opponent of the Bible's account of man's genesis. Kitchen suggests that Patrick's mother who had lost her sight the year before (1873), may well have considered that her youngest son was plunging into another kind of darkness. But Geddes obtained his parents' permission and blessing within a few days, evidence – as Kitchen points out – of both his parents' affection for him and his powers of persuasion (to say nothing of their having the financial means to subsidise him).

In due course, Geddes completed his apprenticeship under Huxley and began to make his own way – but consistently backed by Huxley. In the early part of 1878, Geddes had what he described as 'a sharp illness' and was advised by his doctors to take a holiday out of London. Huxley therefore introduced Geddes to Roscoff and its marine laboratory station, but also to life and learning in France. After that first spring holiday, Geddes returned to work there for the whole summer. Boardman delightfully describes both the effect of Geddes's time in Brittany and his subsequent move to Paris. He researched and published, and learned of new ideas beyond biology, of Frederick le Play and his famous triad: *Travail, Famille, Lieu.*

This period of Geddes's life is often represented as somewhat unsatisfactory, like a student drifting, unsure of where to go next. This was not the case; Geddes had been 'head-hunted'. Someone had brought him forward and he was now sponsored by the British Association for the Advancement of Science.

Patrick Geddes left Paris to go to Naples, but for a purpose, as part of the Aberdeen University project. The Naples model was the standard for marine laboratories at that time and Geddes spent a week there gathering information. The newspaper reports indicate that the adapted drill hall had two apartments. The larger room was closer to the sea and held all the apparatus for the marine station, including trawling gear for collecting specimens and microscopes. It appeared to serve as a marine laboratory and also as a store. The smaller room was used as a zoological library and there were also tanks for public display of marine animals. The Aberdeen zoological station fulfilled all the requirements for a marine laboratory and this was directly as a result of Geddes involvement, with his experience at Roscoff and his fact-finding visit to Naples.

Once the marine station was established, the collecting, recording, dissecting and displays were overseen by Professor Cossar Ewart. The men at the research station made studies on the fish brought in by the fishermen, and in particular, any unusual catch they made. When the research station closed, the weatherglass used by the students was presented to the oldest Cowie fisherman. A newspaper photograph from the 1980s shows the weatherglass still hanging in his daughter's cottage at Cowie. It is unlikely that it was Geddes who undertook the presentation of the weatherglass, as he set sail for Mexico on 10 September and the marine station was not dismantled until later in the year. It was probably fully operational until well into the autumn of 1897. Geddes had little time or opportunity to leave a substantial footprint at Stonehaven; one can imagine, however, that Geddes would have approved of the passing on of the weatherglass to the fisherman, as an acknowledgement of the community's assistance.

The work at Cowie would have suited Patrick Geddes, being a combination of practical outdoor collection on the shore and at sea, and work with academics, students, fishermen and local people. He was teaching and he was learning. He was out in the fresh air, the high skies and the long summer days of the North East of Scotland, in an historical and fascinating landscape. He was part of a pioneering scientific project and he was earning his living doing work that he loved. It is an excellent example of the Geddes motto, *Vivendo Discimus*, 'By Living We Learn'.

Geddes was uniquely placed to deliver the Naples model in Cowie and be then able to continue working at the University of Aberdeen. This, however, was only a resting place, perhaps a time for reflection upon the many exciting theories and ideas he had come across in France. He was exploring other possibilities, including a sponsored trip to Mexico, and applying for the newly formed Chair of Zoology at Queen's College, Manchester. Alternatively, however, he might have felt trapped, back in the more stifling atmosphere of a Scottish university and still in a fairly junior position. In one sense he was no longer needed by the university. He had set up the station, all that was needed for the subsequent moves was to replicate his model elsewhere.

Geddes did not know that his time as a pure scientist was drawing to a close and that he would do little pure laboratory work in the future, due to the repercussions of temporary blindness in Mexico. But he may well have grown restless at Cowie; the work may not have been stimulating or diverse enough for him; it was not, after all, his own project. He had done well. He had set up the station and set it running. No doubt he would be able to look back at his achievement and feel good. No doubt there were decent folk he had met and useful discoveries he had made. Was Cowie the light before the darkness? Was it a period of time which he could draw upon, both when he was blind and in later life in his reflections on the environment and how the world worked?

Mexico

Geddes was awarded £50 from the British Association for the Advancement of Science to conduct palaeontological and zoological research in Mexico. He sailed from Liverpool on 10 September 1879 and one month later arrived in Mexico City, where his brother, Robert, was a banker. He used Robert's house as a base and began collecting crayfish for Huxley, assorted reptiles and crustaceans for the British Museum, and specimens of tropical and semitropical flora for himself. In November his health began to suffer due to overwork. The prescribed treatment of periodic bleedings exacerbated this. At the same time, cumulative eye strain from years of close work at the microscope was brought to a crisis by the excessively bright sunlight. The result was that he was made a blind invalid, sentenced to an indefinite term in a dark room. In despair, his 'thinking machines' provided an outlet for his nervous energies and led him towards a new range of concerns. Fortunately, the physical darkness did not last, but Geddes's sight was permanently impaired as far as long periods of microscope research were concerned.

He returned to Britain, to a period in which he was unable to pursue his chosen career yet could not find a satisfactory alternative. Only in the late 1880s, with his marriage, the start of his Edinburgh social housing ventures and his appointment to Dundee, could the metaphorical darkness be said to have vanished.

The influence of Cowie on Geddes

The marine station at Cowie and Geddes's involvement with it have now been described in detail. This allows an opportunity to examine how this short period in PG's life might have affected his future thoughts and work. Such an analysis has resulted in a plethora of possible influences. They are presented here to promote discussion, perhaps to reinforce what is already known about Geddes, but also to refresh some of the 'received wisdom' about a man of whom so much has already been written. The conclusions fall into six categories, as follows: work, folk, place; learning by doing; the Valley Section; the thinking machine; continuing links with the University of Aberdeen and public exhibitions. Each will be examined in turn.

In Paris he learnt about the work of Frederick Le Play, who applied the methods of scientific field research to society itself. He was particularly interested in the idea that society is conditioned first by geography and then by occupation. He would have found an excellent example of this in the fishing community of Cowie. People lived there to fish and had done so for centuries. In 1879, their lives were still dominated by their ability to catch fish and thus earn a living. It is a simple example of the natural interconnectivity of work, folk and place.

Cowie also offered an excellent example of learning by doing. One wonders what the Cowie residents would have thought of the scientific research station in their midst. The only reports indicate a friendly exchange of ideas and information. Patrick Geddes is unlikely to have been aloof or condescending to the fisher folk. He may well have walked along the shore to explore the change in geology and the start of the Highland Fault. He probably visited the ruins of St Nathan's Church and he may have asked locals about its history. In later years he liked to teach in a garden, having been so taught by his own father at Kinnoull. St Nathan's predilection towards working the land would no doubt have found resonance with him. Much of his time there would have been spent outside: understanding the habitat, finding the specimens and introducing students to the coastal environment and what they could learn from it. He would be learning at the same time as the students, and they would all be learning from the fishermen of Cowie: *Vivendo Discimus* 'By Living We Learn'.

The coastline at Cowie might conceivably also have provided one of the many influences on the visual representation of the Valley Section. This part of the North East of Scotland has a beautiful coastline and one that has not in essence changed since 1879. It has been much reproduced in recent years by artists and photographers. In the course of the research for this chapter, a modern view of Stonehaven with Cowie in the distance was purchased, to act as an *aide-memoire* of the general appearance of the area (PLATE 6B). It was put with other material for this chapter and gradually the writer became aware that the image on the card was startlingly similar to the reproduction of the stained glass panel that was commissioned by Geddes for the Outlook Tower in the 1890s and is on the front cover of *Think Global, Act Local* (PLATE 1). It is regarded as 'the most colourful, the most complex, and one of the most illuminating versions' of the Valley Section. The image of Stonehaven is not like the stained glass panel in every respect, but the coastal areas and the juxtaposing of the harbour and the cliffs are definitely resonant of it. There is the coastal village element from Cowie and the trading element from the harbour at Stonehaven

FIG 9
Stonehaven Harbour, with Cowie Water and shore in distance
(George Washington Wilson Collection, Aberdeen University Library)

(PLATE 6C). This writer would like to believe that Patrick Geddes's inspiration of the coastal element of his commissioned Valley Section, may well have come in some part from his time spent in this part of Kincardine.

His thinking machines were born out of his frustrations in Mexico when he could not see. He would no doubt have drawn on all the visual images of his 26 years, in Perth, Edinburgh, London, Paris, Roscoff, Naples and Mexico. Aubrey Manning, in his opening address to the Geddes Anniversary Exhibition, described the stunning visual experience Geddes must have had at Roscoff, where the flatworms turned the beaches bright green at low tide. Geddes must have recalled this, alternately in despair at the loss of his sight and, optimistically, as he resolved to see them again. He may well have returned in his mind's eye to the walks along the beach at Cowie, which he had undertaken only a few months previously. He may have thought about walking alone and turning over all the sociological theories that had so excited him in Paris. He may have considered the location in which he had so recently been working and reconciled the theory with the practice in the small and relatively straightforward community at Cowie. He may have reflected on the teaching and demonstrating that he undertook in London, Paris and for the University of Aberdeen and begun to work out how the knowledge was imparted and absorbed, and the link between different elements of information and in partic- ular learning. He might well have considered the Aberdeen University students, because he had so recently taught them in particular. Furthermore, he may have had more autonomy there because of the location at the research station and the fact that he was no longer a student demonstrator. His teaching may have been particularly enthused by the steady influx, perhaps even on each tide, of samples and specimens from the sea, by which they worked. It is clear that the medical students appreciated his teaching style and were sorry to lose him. When he went blind, he had to delve within himself to find inner resources to cope with the darkness: the uncertainty of knowing whether he would be cured, plus the depressing effect of the debilitating medical treatments. He had a great deal of resources from which to draw and from these eventually came the thinking machines, which were to influence his teaching for the rest of his life.

Geddes may have looked back at the weeks at Cowie; at the ordered but difficult life of the fisher folk; at the fascinating but, in his case, perhaps not quite exciting enough discoveries at the zoological station, as a time of unappreciated calm and order. He certainly considered Aberdeen the place to which he wanted to return when he was seeking a position after the Mexico trip. It is well documented that he did not obtain a Chair until a part-time one was funded for him at the University of Dundee. He did, however, always retain his links with the University of Aberdeen, in particular in relation to the study of botany and evolution. In fact, his major contribution to scientific writing was done in collaboration with J. Arthur Thompson, a former pupil of his, who succeeded Cossar Ewart to the Chair of Natural History at the University of Aberdeen. Thompson appeared to be able to keep him focused, despite his many and varied other commitments. This may be because of his deep-seated admiration for his former teacher due to the fact that, as Thompson apparently explained to Geddes himself, 'you forced your students to think'. The Cowie period, therefore, was the start of a continuing relationship with the University of Aberdeen, from which flowed the majority of his scientific publications.

Finally, Patrick Geddes is well known for his town planning exhibitions and his desire to involve everyone with his projects. At Cowie, he would undoubtedly have contributed towards the public displays at the marine research station. There was popular interest in the developments of science at that time; Geddes was always a teacher and one eager to engage the public. In 1879, Stonehaven was already a holiday resort. An exhibition at the new zoological station would have been a pleasant destination for a walk by Victorian visitors as well as locals. One can envisage him organising the public displays and encouraging members of the public to come in and look at the exhibits. The work on the scientific displays may well have influenced his future public exhibitions around the world. It is well known that Geddes recognised the importance of engaging the public by way of exhibition and this is an excellent early example.

Concluding Thoughts About Patrick Geddes, Cowie and Modern Scotland

Walking along the beach at Cowie now, one's eye is always drawn to the far horizon and the cliffs which form the opposite shore of Stonehaven Bay. On it stands one of the most poignant war memorials in Scotland. It is a columned circular stone structure, not quite finished, to represent the unfinished lives of those who died. It was erected first to mark the dead of World War 1. Patrick Geddes was 25 when he was at Cowie, unmarried and only just finished student life himself. In 1879, the Zulu War was being fought in Africa, but the horrors of World War 1 and the death of his own oldest son, Alasdair, could not have been imagined. The War Memorial was not to be erected for some 40 years after Geddes's time at Cowie; it is, however, so perfect in the landscape, it is hard to imagine this coastline without it. Patrick Geddes was a pacifist and a pragmatist, so often frustrated by the resort to a war in his lifetime. Nothing can ever compensate for the loss of a son, but perhaps he might have approved of this fitting marriage of man-made structure and landscape in the Stonehaven war memorial; one that truly illustrates the folly of war.

He would also be horrified to discover that the beach at Cowie could certainly not be used for a marine research station in 2006. It consistently fails European standards for bathing waters, being one of only three sites in Scotland to do so, as a result of untreated sewage being pumped out to sea. Scottish Water recently obtained approval from the Scottish Executive to construct a screening plant at Cowie, but this was only after a hard fought battle, with the local community in the village uniting to object and put forward an alternative proposal. This was not a good example of community engagement or inclusive planning and the very fact that the site of the first marine research station in Great Britain is now highly contaminated is an indictment of all public bodies concerned.

Patrick Geddes would, however, be highly interested in the development of the concept of marine spatial planning, a planning system for the sea. At the time of writing, in England and Wales a draft bill is being consulted upon by DEFRA, with a view to legislation being introduced at Westminster in 2007. The Scottish Executive is also exploring marine spatial planning for the waters around Scotland and a marine national park for Scotland is anticipated by 2008.

Sir Patrick Geddes's legacy continues to grow and at last Scotland is truly recognising the worth of his thinking in relation to planning and sustainable development. An excellent recent example is in the introduction to the Scottish Executive's white paper, 'Modernising Planning' June 2004:

> We want our planning system to return to the vision of Patrick Geddes, the Scot who is the father of town planning, who saw the need for a system that balanced the needs of 'folk, work and place'... Patrick Geddes saw how the way we live affects everything around us, we know that this is still the case and we need a modern planning system that helps us to plan for the way we live now.

At the time of writing, the Planning (Scotland) Bill 2005 is being debated in the Scottish Parliament. Whatever Patrick Geddes might think about government and the statutory planning system that has evolved over the last 60 years in Scotland, one must imagine that he would delight in the location of the Scottish Parliament, at the end of the Royal Mile, in the Old Town of Edinburgh, just across the street from one of his essays in conservative surgery.

Miss Geddes's Dresden Establishment

Walter Stephen

AS THE WIFE of Patrick Geddes, Anna Geddes has rightly received a great deal of attention and admiration. Anna Morton (1857–1917) became Patrick Geddes's wife in 1886 and was to become the mother of their three children. She shared many of his ventures and some of his enthusiasms. Through his long absences and frequent changes of residence she kept the family together and its father on course. Geddes was frequently on the edge of bankruptcy and Anna was the rock on which he was able to build his creative life.

We know, not least from PG himself, what were the early influences on Geddes's life and thought. A main source for Anna Morton's background is Philip Mairet, who makes it clear in his introduction to *The Life and Letters of Patrick Geddes* that Arthur and Norah Geddes, Anna and Patrick's surviving children, had complete confidence in him as a biographer and had freely placed in his hands personal papers and family letters, giving him real freedom of selection and final judgment.

Arthur, writing 40 years after his mother's death, wrote:

Patrick and Anna, man and wife, achieved and maintained success through all their adventures together and apart. Without Anna, without the intimate relationship they made together, Patrick's flashes of discovery might have lacked the fire which sustained thought and civic action. Without her he could not have dwelt so continuously nor with such understanding in the sick core of the Old Town. A great-hearted man with many faults, he could not have attained his moral stature without her ardour of love, faith, and clear-eyed critique. She too felt herself fortunate, in spite of the difficulties of sharing so nomadic a life, so many anxieties and risks. Anxious friends frequently condemned the risks; but the decisions were shared. And Anna, as musician, kept ready to resume teaching if need be, as her valued friend Marjory Kennedy-Fraser had done when left a widow. She knew that, should the worst befall, she could face the future. Her children knew only that she played and sang for her own sake and theirs and because she loved it.

Amelia Defries, while Geddes was still alive, wrote of the Exposition Internationale at Ghent in 1913. PG arrived late, but fortunately:

> His wife came with him, the calm grey-haired lady who could bring order out of chaos.
> Even more valuable... was her power of intercession, her ability to tone down Pat's cerebral high-voltage when some bewildered soul was in danger of electrocution.

As Miss Defries said:

> Mrs Geddes found time, while sorting books and jotting down notes, to enquire as to my health and living arrangements; and a few days later she had me in much better rooms, working shorter hours and living more normally than during the last three months.

Clearly this was a marriage of true minds and they continued to write each other love letters for all of their married lives. Yet there is a suggestion that they were so close and so busy that the efficient organisation of the children left little space for 'over-flowing mother-love', as Arthur phrased it, or, as Paddy Kitchen suggests, the constant need for discipline quelled spontaneity and the expression of personal instincts. Anna had 'her full share of moral earnestness'.

> Both were moved by the new spirit of social service and both had a streak of puritan severity in their idealism. Their rejection of the religious ideas of their parents did not incline them to laxity in self-discipline; it made them rather less tolerant of self-indulgence, sometimes in others as well as in themselves.

Thus says Philip Mairet.
Even Alasdair, loyal, courageous, trustworthy Alasdair, could say: 'no human being could live as well as work with PG and survive'. Yet

Anna survived for over 30 years of marriage and, at the end, Geddes felt he had to use subterfuge to conceal Alasdair's death from her, to spare her one last blow. When PG's own parents died, it was Anna who was with them and carried out the formalities of registration.

When she married, Anna was 28, rather old for a Victorian bride, and quite a blue-stocking. How did she get to this point? Her father, Frazer Morton, an Ulster Scot, was a prosperous textile merchant in Liverpool and a strict Presbyterian. He had strong opinions, not least on the conduct of young ladies. Even jumping or climbing were taboo and only the mother's relatively easy attitude softened the home atmosphere. Yet Morton had a hidden weakness: he learned – in secret – how to play the violin, so that music became the one indulgence permitted in his family. We are told that Anna was a highly educated young lady of great intelligence, not beautiful but with great personal charm. Her school was known for its polite learning, with its 'Italian and the use of the globes'.

At 18 she studied music for a year at Dresden, where, heavily fathered but liberally educated, she became the first of her family to go through the painful experience of having to break away from the Church. After Dresden, she took up music teaching and set up her own girls' club near the family home in Liverpool. The desire to render social service led her into contact with Octavia Hill, Josephine Butler and others, although no opportunity arose for her to work with them in London. She was also involved in the incipient movement for the emancipation of women.

Anna's younger sister, Edith, had married a James Oliphant, headmaster of the Charlotte Square (Edinburgh) Institution for the education of girls, and a friend of Geddes. Another sister, Rebecca, married Peter Dott, an art dealer, and settled in Colinton, then a picturesque village outside the town. On a visit from Liverpool, Anna attended some of the Oliphants' evening get-togethers on social problems and later wrote to Geddes. PG, Oliphant and the Morton sisters were founder members of the 'Environmental Society' in 1884. A correspondence developed in 1885 until, on a Sunday early in 1886, Geddes proposed to Anna in the Royal Botanic Garden. In a typically Geddes touch, although the gardens were closed to the public – it being the Sabbath – he had access to them.

Anna and Patrick were married in her parents' home in Egremont, Liverpool on 17 April 1886.

Music and Dresden were obviously important in Anna's life; so let us pause for a moment to consider the significance of Dresden in the 1870s. The revolutionary activities of 1848 were long over. The German Empire had just been formed, so that Saxony had ceased to be a separate state. Yet Dresden retained all the trappings of one of the richest capitals of Europe.

> Dresdeners of all classes thought they lived in one of the most beautiful, cultured and well-administered cities in... Europe... [in a] seemingly unchanging backdrop of time-honoured beauty combined with judicious modernity.

This they were happy to share with foreign residents and tourists. Writing of a slightly later period, Frederick Taylor states that:

> Compared with foreigners resident in Dresden, the Jews were a fairly small group, outnumbered by the four thousand or more British and American residents.

Many of them were like Anna Morton and Agnes Tillie, whom we now meet.

Agnes Tillie was the eldest child of William Tillie (1823–1904), of Tillie and Henderson, whose huge shirt factory, with a workforce of 4,500 and the largest in the world, dominated the Craigavon Bridge over the Foyle at Londonderry until it was demolished in 2005.

William Tillie, born in Crookston (Midlothian), was a farmer's son who learned the textile business in Glasgow before moving to Londonderry in 1851 – by no means the only Borderer to do so. In 1852, he was the first manufacturer to introduce the sewing machine into industrial processing, ensuring half a century of rapid growth and another half-century of edgy prosperity. He was a major figure in the First Derry Presbyterian Church and had many philanthropic outlets. Of his many public offices, the most notable was His Majesty's Lieutenant for the City of Londonderry. A final accolade – Karl Marx cited the good practices at the Foyle Factory in *Das Kapital*.

FIG 10
The Tillie and Henderson factory in the late 1960s
(Waterside Voices)

His wife, Agnes, also involved herself in charitable enterprises, chief of which was her interest in providing nursing for the working classes. As vice president and founding member of the Londonderry District Nursing Society, she personally financed a fully equipped district nurses' home in Great James Street (in the congested industrial area of the city).

Of the Tillie family of eight, daughter Agnes (the eldest) and the second daughter both married clergymen. The eldest son, William J. Tillie, managed the Glasgow branch of the family firm, although often in poor health, until taking over at Londonderry from 1915 to 1928. Twins Alexander and Marshall, were educated at the Academical Institution, Londonderry (probably as day boys). This, while they were at school, became Foyle College – the Londonderry public school of which their father was a governor. Alexander went on to the Park School, Glasgow, Glasgow University 'and abroad' before setting up a linen-manufacturing firm in Belfast. He settled permanently in London, establishing another branch there and accumulating senior positions in the City.

Marshall attended the International College in Passy, Paris for a year, before taking his place in the family firm. After his father's death he took over the management of Foyle Factory and added the Abercorn Factory, with a further 1,200 workers. Like his father, he accumulated a string of public offices. At his death, he was, as his father had been, Lieutenant for the City.

In 1872, Agnes Tillie wrote to her friend, Jane (Jenny) Cooke describing some of her experiences at a finishing school in Dresden run by a Miss Geddes, Jenny came from Ramelton, Co Donegal and was to marry David Cleghorn Hogg, another Borderer from near Galashiels. Her grandson, Arthur Hogg (formerly of Hogg and Mitchell, whose former shirt factory in Great James Street, Londonderry has been well restored as ground-floor shops with flats above) uncovered Agnes's letter and has very kindly permitted its reproduction here.

Miss Geddes
21 Walpurgis Strasse
Dresden
Feb 3rd, 1872

My dearest Jenny,

It is now more than a fortnight since I learned of your engagement to my cousin and yet this is the first day I have found time to write you a note of congratulation. But my good wishes are none the less hearty for being thus delayed, and I am very glad indeed that your future life will probably be in Derry so that we shall see one another much oftener than we have generally been able to do since we were at school together.

I know how happy you must be feeling just now, if your experience is like mine of this time last year, and I can fancy how the happiness will, in your case also, settle down after the first excitement has passed into a most perfect contentment and satisfaction. And I am sure it will be so with you, dear Jenny, for I remember how you used to say 'one must love a man very much before she would marry him'. But what has become of all your fine speeches about being an old maid and all that.

Aha! Miss Jenny, didn't I tell you? And you used to shake your head so gravely too, and look so wise whenever I assured you that your turn would come next and very soon too.

I shall be going home in three months more, and the time has gone so quickly since I came that I can hardly believe it is five months since. Heavens. I have been very fortunate in finding such a pleasant and I hope profitable home among strangers. I can speak German now better than French but not yet read it so well, and I have very good music and singing lessons. There are a good many of us here, almost forty including one or two day-boarders. Most of my schoolfellows are Scotch, a few English, but we are obliged to speak French and German in alternate months and English only on Sundays. Miss Geddes takes us to a great many delightful concerts, and occasionally to the opera and theatre, which I enjoy immensely.

Of course I am very busy. You know well enough what a boarding school life is, how monotonous, how full of work, how every week looks like another, and how they fly past. We had a pleasant time of rest and change for a week at Christmas, and Easter is coming soon, to bring the summer again, and then when the year is at its brightest and bonniest, in the sweet May-time, I am going home.

Mama did not mention if there was any time fixed for the consummation of your engagement but I hope it will not be long postponed. Meantime, accept my most earnest wishes for your future happiness and

Believe me as ever,
Your loving friend, Agnes M. Tillie

Agnes Tillie's background was similar to Anna Morton's and her experiences were also likely to be the same as Anna's. We think of the prosperous Victorian as a stern *paterfamilias*, ruling his dull conformist household with a rod of iron. Yet both sets of parents sought improvement, social and intellectual, for their children and were happy to release them – in suitably controlled circumstances.

We can see Miss Geddes's establishment as a 'finishing school' concerned with appearances only, but Anna emerged from her 'gap year' capable of supporting herself as a teacher of music.

Writing three years before Anna Morton's residence in Dresden, Agnes Tillie's letter gives at least an inkling of what the city had to offer as preparation for a full life. Unfortunately, since both Jenny and she had had experience of life at boarding school she didn't feel the need to give a full picture of life at Miss Geddes's establishment. But she gave the size of the place – almost 40 students – with one or two day-pupils but mostly boarders. Of them, most were from Scotland; the few English (and Irish) probably had Scottish connections. The curriculum was a liberal one, with specialisation in music and the modern languages of French and German. Social education was built round concerts and the theatre.

Although Anna Morton was in Dresden three years after Agnes Tillie, the finishing schools were limited in number and would have shared the same kinds of activity, perhaps even the same teachers – of music, for example. So Anna would have known of Miss Geddes's establishment by repute and might even have met some of the girls from there. Her prosperous father's Ulster Scots textile background certainly matched Agnes Tillie's. Anna had her full share of moral earnestness, which Agnes clearly shared. Agnes emerges from the page as a thoroughly nice girl. It comes as no surprise to learn that she later married the minister of First Derry Presbyterian Church, as hinted at in her letter.

It would be satisfying to be able to establish a connection between Patrick Geddes and Miss Geddes of Walpurgis Strasse, but 'Geddes' is a common enough name in Scotland – for example, the Edinburgh telephone directory has about 100 Geddeses – and many Scottish women in the 19th century managed schools, hospitals, lunatic asy-lums and the like – in many countries.

It would be even more satisfying to be able to establish that Anna had attended Miss Geddes's establishment and to have discovered more detail about the life and curriculum there. There is quite a list of organ-isations whose records might be expected to help (see Bibliography), but the obstacles to research are many. The terrible events of February 1945 destroyed so much that it would be naïve to expect the survival of papers relating to an obscure private school. Walpurgis Strasse itself was devastated and the site has been replaced with pleasant garden flats (PLATE 7).

As Edinburgh has the National Library of Scotland and the Edinburgh City Libraries, so Dresden has sources based on the city, but also on the former kingdom of Saxony and the present Land of Sachsen. Amazingly, enough similar material did survive to raise hopes that still more might be found, although this researcher must have seemed, at times, like the reporter who said: 'But apart from that, Mrs Lincoln, how did you enjoy the play?' At all times people in Dresden have been patient and polite, while some have shown support beyond the call of duty. Nevertheless, the project remains at an unsatisfactory state. We have two lives, broadly similar and very close at one stage, but making a connection may well be impossible.

One relevant piece of evidence was found, in a contemporary street directory. Under 'Walpurgis Strasse' we note that numbers 9 to 11 are still under construction, showing that the street as a whole is brand-new, between the old town and the suburban Grosser Garten with its Zoological Garden. No 21, like all the other houses, is a big six-decker block of flats (basement, parterre and four more floors). What we would call the rateable value is given. From this we can tell that No 21 was the second-largest, second-best in the street – perhaps the best, since No 17 was slightly bigger but had many more occupants listed.

If the young ladies were permitted to promenade to the Grosser Garten, whom were they likely to meet on the way? Many of the residents would have been listed in the Census of Scotland as 'Living on Private Means' or 'Annuitant'. There were some military gentlemen, a lieutenant-general, a major-general and several majors. Ward was Consul-General, probably British or American. A baron lived in No 5 and a baroness (unrelated) in No 13. Senior officials abounded – police registrar, accident inspector, advocates, notaries, bankers, financiers and the like. There were a few doctors, a dentist, a dietitian and an architect.

Trade was well represented, detailed entries indicating that Walpurgis Strasse was the place of residence and that the business was carried on in the old town. Presumably most of these tradesmen – merchants and masters – had lived 'over the shop' but had now risen to prosperity and the suburbs. A sprinkling of quite lowly occupations seem to have located themselves on the top floors. These included a postman, a city policeman, a gardener, a lithographer, a corset-finisher, two house-painters, a seamstress and a glove-maker. This is reminiscent of the social stratification of the tenements in the Old Town of Edinburgh. In Walpurgis Strasse there lived 15 'vons', three on the ground floor, five on the first floor, six on the second, one on the third. No aristocrat lived in a basement or on the fourth floor.

What of the Dresden Anna and Agnes had been sent to benefit from? There were teachers galore, of all sorts; a PhD in the *Gymnasium*, another teaching maths, language teachers, male and female. Hugo Zegler Jnr was a journalist and language teacher, his wife a pianoforte teacher. On the third floor of No 8 lived an actor. On the top floor of No 1 was an instrument maker and singer (one person). Herr Mansfeldt, music director, shared the ground floor of No 14 with a major and a merchant.

No 21 itself shows the social stratification we have just noted. In the basement was Herr Rollbed, living on private means (we can be sure that the girls had a giggle over his name). On the ground floor were a merchant, an optician and a dealer in ribbons and fine goods. On the fourth floor were a master tailor for men, another (unrelated) master tailor and an office worker.

That leaves the first, second and third floors of No 21. Nowhere else in the street is more than one flat used by one occupant, but these three floors are occupied thus:

Geddes Margaret, Rentiére
Geddes, Jane, Rentiére
Maczyneta, Gräfin

What are we to make of this? Not one Miss Geddes, but two. And living with an exotic-sounding (Polish?) countess across three vast floors. And no mention of the 'almost 40' girls. As we shall see below, Dresden had planning controls and a school was probably not an appropriate land use in this new suburb. The sisters – one perhaps dominant and outgoing, the other quiet but hard-working – no doubt had invested their capital (their inheritance?) in what had become their home and had registered it accordingly. The countess was probably down on her luck and had become, in effect, a paying guest. Her presence would have lent some lustre to the establishment and she would have been an excellent mentor on the niceties of polite behaviour.

In this situation, the historical novelist has no problem. There is a structure of known people and events. To invent a couple of characters who can be made to frequent real locations and intertwine with real people in an atmosphere of turmoil, intrigue or menace would be quite easy; easier than the dull business of disinterring the truth. Like Sir Walter Scott, one could make the sun set in the east (as in *The Antiquary*) or produce marvellous descriptions of the Alps on no more basis than Salvator Rosa's drawings (as in *Anne of Geierstein*).

At Hellerau, just north of Dresden, the first Garden City on the English model in Germany was founded in 1898. In 1911 the Fest-spielhaus opened, to become the home of Dalcroze and the Eurhythmics movement. A.S. Neill, ex-headmaster of Gretna Green School, author of the *Dominie* books and leading light in the progressive education movement, helped to set up the International School at Hellerau in 1921. For the very first chapter of his mighty *World's End* series of novels, amounting to over a million words, Upton Sinclair describes a set-piece symbolic of the spirit of optimism and brotherhood prevalent in the Europe of 1913. Three fictitious teenagers, whose fortunes we will follow for the next 30 or so years, perform Dalcroze eurhythmics in the Festspielhaus at Hellerau. This was a real event in a real place; those the youngsters met – Stanislawsky and George Bernard Shaw – were real people (as were Le Corbusier (architecture), Kafka (literature), Kokoscha (art), Rachmaninov (music), who were also there). But the insertion of three fictional characters, one German, one British and one American resident in France, gave Sinclair the latitude to fill in the spaces between the facts with imaginative reconstruction (PLATE 8A). To the 'tall white temple... were drifting throngs of people who had journeyed from places all over the earth where art was loved and cherished'. *World's End* and its successors, through a mix of real and imagined people, simply chronicle the puncturing of idealism and the triumph of state-directed brutality in two world wars.

It is hardly possible for us to say to what extent Dresden featured in the home life of the Geddes family. What did the family discuss at the breakfast table? Certainly the home was filled with music. Anna led and all the children played. Did Anna ever reminisce about her student days in 'Florence on the Elbe'? Or compare the old gentlemen the finishing school girls used to see at the opera or the public gardens with the eager idealists of Hellerau and the Festspielhaus? Geddes was always pro-French and, if not anti-German, he was certainly against Prussian militarism. Did he work out his attitudes single-handedly, or was Anna the opinion-former?

From 24 May to 7 June 1911, Geddes's Cities and Town Planning Exhibition was held in Dublin. One section was called 'Great Germanic Cities', one of them being Dresden. According to the catalogue: 'The Town Plans of Dresden show that the city has been in steady development for thirty years.' (That is, since Agnes and Anna's time.) The zones of the city are shown in different colours and reflect the controlling Building Order, e.g. factories allowed, provided the chimneys do not exceed a certain height. There is nothing in the catalogue to suggest that Geddes had ever been in Dresden or had talked informally about the city.

In the autumn of 1912, Alasdair and Patrick went on a tour of German cities. Geddes could not have been ignorant of Hellerau and its importance in the spread of new urban ideas. He would have been duty bound to go and see for himself. To what extent was it a sentimental journey, revisiting Anna's haunts vicariously?

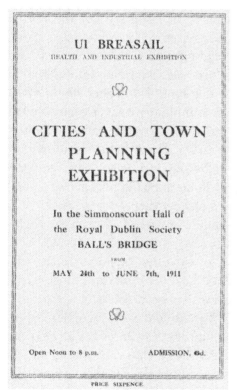

FIG 11
Cities and Town Planning Catalogue,
Dublin 1911 – cover

UI BREASAIL
HEALTH AND INDUSTRIAL EXHIBITION

CITIES AND TOWN
PLANNING
EXHIBITION

In the Simmonscourt Hall of
the Royal Dublin Society
BALL'S BRIDGE
FROM
MAY 24th to JUNE 7th, 1911

Open Noon to 8 p.m.   ADMISSION, 6d.

PRICE SIXPENCE

Particularly because Alasdair was there also, it is inconceivable that the two men were not primed as to what to see and where to go.

Were this essay fiction it would be possible to set up an Old Wives' Tale, in which the two young friends separate to live contrasting lives, to be reunited in old age. But in the prevailing murk around the Dresden episode, one fact remains. When Anna Geddes first heard the name 'Patrick Geddes', or was first introduced to him, perhaps at her sister's home, it would not have been a name completely unfamiliar to her. It would have had resonances associated with Miss Geddes of Dresden, with her establishment, with the city itself and with the kind of girl who went there – 'one of our sort', but in the nicest possible way.

Patrick and Anna were off to a good start.

Through a Glass, Clearly

Behind the Photographs of the First Survey of Edinburgh by Patrick Geddes

Sofia Leonard

WHEN I WAS CALLED in 1985 to help with the Geddes Archives at the recently-created Patrick Geddes Centre for Planning Studies, I found among the masses of documents, maps, globes and models at the Outlook Tower, a drawer full of loosely piled dark glass negatives. Some were in three small original boxes and had survived in very good condition. The majority, lying loose, were in individual envelopes. Others had no protective envelope or identification or just lay in an assortment of broken pieces of glass in another box. Many loose slides had started to deteriorate and a few had been attacked by fungus.

What did they contain? Who took the photographs and what was their purpose?

These were the questions that came immediately to mind. There wasn't an easy answer. In fact it took several years to have a complete set of positives to work from. Only then could the very fragile glass negatives be put away in new acid free envelopes and the process of identification he started.

Dry glass plate slides were new technology in photography at the time of Geddes, and were mostly used for amusement and entertainment. However, Geddes used their great potential in an innovative way for his first planning survey of Edinburgh. The glass slides found languishing at the bottom of a drawer had indeed played a vital role in the work towards the regeneration of Edinburgh's Old Town by Patrick Geddes, as we will see later.

Geddes burst into the Edinburgh scene in 1884 while in his early thirties. He soon involved himself in the renewal movement through his connections with the Secular Positivist debating group. Members of this group were Dr and Mrs Glasse of the Greyfriars Church and James Oliphant, then headmaster of the Charlotte Square Institution for the education of girls. James was married to Edith Morton, daughter of Frazer Morton, a Liverpool merchant originally from Northern Ireland. Looking through the 'Transactions of the Edinburgh Photographic Society' of March 1892 I saw that James Oliphant had been vice chairman and an active member of the photographic society, so he would have been well acquainted with the techniques and uses of photography.

In 1884 Geddes, Oliphant, the Morton sisters Edith, Anna and Rebecca and Frank Deas among others were founder members of the Environmental Society. In 1886 Anna married Geddes, coming to live with him in Edinburgh, and joining and fully participating in the activities of the society. This original group soon evolved into the better known group called the 'Edinburgh Social Union'. Their immediate aim was:

> ...to make the best of present conditions and to raise the standard of comfort of the local people...

They set out to do something about the unwholesomeness of the homes of the poor and to provide opportunities for healthy enjoyment, higher tastes and pleasures by a process of aid and example.

There are similarities with the methods of Canon Samuel Barnett (1844–1913) working in Whitechapel in London, and the work of Octavia Hill whose activities were deeply admired by Anna Morton even before her marriage.

Patrick and Anna chose to live in James Court, in the Old Town of Edinburgh, among the people of the Lawnmarket area. For them, he developed a method for Regeneration, aiming to turn a downward spiral of degradation and despair into an upward spiral of hope.

How did he achieve such a feat, a model for the world?

He believed that dereliction and degradation are man-created, therefore he was sure that regeneration could be man-directed. Armed with this conviction, with all the zeal of his young years and the unconditional support of his new wife, he set for himself the real objective for any planner:

> ...To improve the living conditions and standard of life of the inhabitants of their town.

He believed also that, as in war, a strategy was needed to fight for regeneration. In order to win, the attack had to be concerted, systematic and sustained. The method he developed and tested on the ground, first in Edinburgh's Old Town, and then later in India, is his best legacy for planners everywhere.

The First Planning Survey of Edinburgh

The starting point for the strategy was to carry out a careful diagnostic survey before taking action. Therefore, the first planning survey of Edinburgh took shape over many years at the Outlook Tower. There he developed his ideas before testing them in the Old Town.

This enquiry, he said, required first a survey of geographical environment in its fullest and deepest aspects: '...for the natural environment should never be neglected without long-enduring penalties.' Secondly, it required:

> ...a survey also of the history... not as mere archaeology, but as the determination of the present from the past...

> ...historic phases cannot be considered as past and done with; for their heritage of good, their burden of evil, each are traceable in our complex present City...

Further, the role of the city has to be fully understood in the context of its region:

> ...From the very outset of our survey of a city we must observe and understand it in its region.

> We cannot trace our City from its early beginnings upon the Castle Rock without understanding it as a hill-fort associated with a sea-port, as well as with the agricultural plain of the Lothian...

> This combination of an Acropolis with its Piraeus and its Attica is common throughout Mediterranean Europe, though

less frequent in the North. Thus we see the traditional comparison of Edinburgh with Athens has really little to do with our eighteen and nineteenth century imitations of Greek temples ... but lies deeper, in geographical and historical origins...

The Survey of Edinburgh and its region seeks to connect our studies of contemporary conditions with their origins... that is the determination of the present by the past; and the tracing of this process in the phases of transformation, progressive or degenerative which our city has exhibited throughout its various periods of development...

In his address at the Geddes Anniversary Symposium, Aubrey Manning stressed the fundamental importance of the biologist in Geddes. He approached the study of human settlements with a scientific mind, in the same way as he would have approached a botanical survey; except that the problem is, of course, larger, because human beings have more complex interactions with their environment, involving psychic and other forces, such as sociological characteristics, level of education, etc. which are not relevant in the study of plants.

For a botanist like Geddes it was obvious that plants required specific environmental conditions or habitat in order to flourish. In a botanical scientific survey it is customary to start by making detailed observations of the whole area, recording on a map the distribution of types of vegetation and their associations. This will be seen in relation to the climate, the setting and soil conditions. A search for past distribution of plants is then correlated with geology and earlier geographical and climatic changes in order to arrive at a dynamic conception of the stock of vegetation.

Geddes's City Survey is in fact an extension and an adaptation of the botanic scientific survey to people living in cities, interpreting the observations of the present in the light of the past and even discovering something of the opening future '...for the future is already incipient, as next season's buds are already here.'

Since, in plants and animals, evolutionary forces dictate that one generation communicates itself to the next, Geddes knew that in humans, civilization's evolutionary transmission is reflected in history.

Therefore, history is of great importance as we must seek the roots of the present in the past. The tracing of the process of change and the identification of the phases of this change are essential for the better understanding of the present and can even allow us to glimpse something of the future. This link with the past, the recognition of trends, the understanding of the problems and identifying of the possibilities for the future is the diagnostic element of the survey which many cities now ignore or are shy to attempt.

Geddes's City Survey is a dynamic model which requires the assistance of all the sciences to encompass the triad of Place, Work, Folk in the past, present and future. He anticipates that a detailed and comprehensive survey of this kind is necessarily difficult and laborious, but not insuperable. He anticipates also that many will hesitate to undertake or even encourage such surveys, which might delay sometimes urgent work.

Working closely with Frank C. Mears, who was later to become his son-in-law, he built up the case study of Edinburgh as a demonstration of how to make a diagnostic city survey of the kind he was advocating. Fortunately, most of the original survey of Edinburgh survives in Edinburgh University Library.

To illustrate Geddes's ideas, Mears made several remarkable drawings by showing the important phases in the development of Edinburgh, over several critical historical periods.

The Mears drawings were complemented, for the Edinburgh Survey, by maps, paintings, models, and by a set of photographs, depicting mainly street scenes, some of which have survived, as we have seen – these are the main concern of this paper. The use of photographs in the survey is an innovation for this period and an eye opener not only for ordinary people but especially for local authorities and other influential organisations.

Action for regeneration

Once the survey was made, Geddes involved himself in the work of regeneration, especially through the Edinburgh Social Union connections. The union was organised in 'Ruskinian' Guilds.

The first was the Artistic Guild. Led by John Duncan, it was later to become the Old Edinburgh School of Art. The guild's aim was to beautify interiors and exteriors in the Old Town. Much of its work survives, especially in the murals of Ramsay Garden, and in *The Evergreen*, the northern seasonal published by Geddes and Colleagues at the Outlook Tower in 1896/7 and edited by William Sharp (alias Fiona McLeod).

The second was the Educational Programme, organised by James Oliphant and offering training and work skills to adolescents from the Castlehill School, with the support of the school board.

The third was the Entertainment Committee, aiming to provide healthy enjoyments such as music and poetry, as opposed to the 'brawling and boozing' that were the spare time occupations of the urban poor. Led by Anna Morton and Marjorie Kennedy-Fraser, the committee organised music and poetry evenings at the Outlook Tower.

The fourth was the Public Open Spaces Committee, chaired by Frank Mears who surveyed all available open space, amid the Old Town slums. These amounted to no less than 75 small 'pieces', measuring about 10 acres in all. On moderate means and with the help of ordinary folk and local children, about a dozen were converted into gardens accessible to school and street children, to women and to people generally. Others, it was hoped, could also be converted depending on circumstances and as scanty funds would allow.

The photographs shown here depict one of these gardens in the process of being cleared. FIG 12 is the space in its original state.

FIG 13 shows the same location, having been made into a garden by the local children under the direction of members of the committee. Clearly, the pairing of these photographs is not just a record of what has happened, but an exhortation to the viewer to go and do likewise.

The dozen or so of these derelict sites made into inner city gardens brought life into the previously stark and dreary alleys of the Old Town. The committee also distributed bulbs to be planted in people's balconies. The Old Town came to life as Geddes had predicted: '...let endure, and plant again the fragrant closes. Their children's children shall have roses.'

Last but not least, the Housing Guild was where Geddes had most direct action and influence. This was also the link between Geddes and the Edinburgh Architectural Association, which he had joined in 1884.

FIG 12
Children's Garden, Johnston Terrace
What a daunting, dreary, dismal place. Note background.
(Patrick Geddes Archive, University of Edinburgh)

His first lecture for the EAA was called rather modestly, 'A Layman's View of Architecture'. Among the members of the association at the time were: Hippolyte Blanc, Thomas Ross (of MacGibbon and Ross), Rowand Anderson, and the University's Professor of Fine Art, Baldwin

FIG 13
Children's Garden, Johnston Terrace
Note background and transformation. Girls in best clothes,
boy in handed-down outfit, genially supervised by a lady with hat,
member of the Public Open Spaces Committee.
(Patrick Geddes Archive, University of Edinburgh)

Brown. One of the founder members of the EAA was George Aitken
(1836–1921), who had a practice in Dundee, and he became a close
collaborator of Geddes, including in the work for the Dunfermline
Report and later in Geddes's proposals for the Royal Mile. Aitken and
Geddes were responsible for the conservation of Lady Stair's House;
now the Writers' Museum, then in danger of demolition.

At this stage, Geddes was able to link his biological repertoire with
the stylistic concerns of his new associates, especially George Aitken and
Henbest Capper. Aitken was very much in the classical Beaux Arts tradition and Capper was interested in romanticism and Art Nouveau.

Geddes wanted also to improve the conditions of the poorly
lodged students of Edinburgh University and the Watt Institute. As
part of his strategy for regeneration he wanted to attract new people
to the Old Town, and he set about providing accommodation for the
students in what he called University Halls.

His first renewal project for this purpose started with the purchase of: 'three commonplace little flats in one of the less favourable situations in the dilapidated Old Town', on the top floor of an 18th century tenement on Mound Place, near James Court, where he himself had established residence. There Geddes installed seven students in study bedrooms, a common kitchen, a dining room and a drawing room – and Scotland had its first student residence.

The history of the buildings in Mound Place is complex. They changed hands several times. They were taken over by the Town and Gown Association in 1903 and renamed Lister House. Later, they were taken over by New College, from 1914 to 1952. Finally, after extensive structural improvements, Lister House was taken over by the university and formally opened by HRH the Duke of Edinburgh, renaming it Patrick Geddes Hall in 1978.

Geddes also rehabilitated accommodation in Bank Street, naming it Blackie House in honour of the Professor of Classics of Edinburgh University. Sydney Henbest Capper gave it its characteristic Arts and Crafts treatment in 1894 with three vertical stacks of bay windows linked by panelling, harled and painted, and with a bust of Blackie in a medallion. Geddes's action in the Lawnmarket led to a rapid increase in student accommodation – a gain in new people living in the centre of town.

Soon he acquired Riddle's Court for the university halls extension. Riddle's Court was a decaying historic property in multiple ownership and occupation and badly in need of sanitary upgrading. From the beginning, the university halls were to be self-governing, in contrast with the paternalistic English collegiate system – a characteristically Scottish decision reflecting Geddes's motto '*Vivendo Discimus*'; inscribed in the stone arch of Riddle's Court. Originally the halls were intended only for young men, but soon they were available also for young women. This was a pioneering action way ahead of time and was viewed with admiration by some and disapproval by others.

The Social Union's Housing Guild gradually built up a fund by managing property for owners and organising rent collection by volunteers. Any surplus of rent, beyond letting expenses and the five per cent interest payable on the capital, was put in a fund for renovation of the property. The Guild became very successful with this method.

In its heyday it had about £100,000 invested in a rolling fund to pro-vide housing improvements in Edinburgh. The breakthrough came with the passing of the Housing of the Working Classes (Scotland) Act of 1890. Geddes, then in high standing in architectural circles, and with the town council, was asked to manage the Lawnmarket area, one of the 10 areas designated for improvements under the improvement scheme approved by the town council.

Thus Geddes, with the boost of new funding, was able to contin-ue with his work in conservative surgery, a method which involved renovating and upgrading most sites capable of renovation with a minimum of demolition. To him conservative surgery (to be applied later in India) was better, less disruptive and a cheaper option than wholesale redevelopment. He was the administrator and manager of the scheme, but the actual design and site supervision in projects such as Blackie House, Wardrop's Court, Riddle's Court and Lady Stair's House was carried out by the architects George Aitken, Henbest Capper and Sidney Mitchell.

The Crudelius University Hall for lady students was opened in Burns' Land (457 Lawnmarket) in Wardrop's Court. (Mary Crudelius, née McLean, 1839–77, was a British campaigner for women's education who lived in Leith in the 1860s and 1870s. She was also a supporter of women's suffrage). Geddes was aware of the difficulties experi-enced by women in finding suitable accommodation, having tutored some women who were not allowed to enrol to study medicine at the University. The hall was completed in 1892. The fruit of a close col-laboration between Geddes and Capper, it was arguably one of the earliest manifestations of the Arts and Crafts movement in Edinburgh. Capper used here the same dominant design feature – that of bay win-dows – as in Blackie House, with exposed timbers in the gables and originally, according to an existing drawing in the Geddes collection, cream and white rendering. The brackets below the windows are carved as heads; an architect, a woman and a boy scholar complete with school bag, as described in *Dramatisations of History* by PG (see FIG 2). The street entrance to the pend is flanked by mythical beasts functioning as brackets, similar to those used in the projecting bal-cony window of the Geddes flat in Ramsay Gardens.

It was at this stage, in 1892, that Geddes acquired the Outlook

Tower. The Tower was to become Geddes's most significant building. The fabric needed very little work. Its location at the top of the Royal Mile and the camera obscura installed in the roof by its previous owner, allowed him to convert it into his headquarters and it became the powerhouse of his regeneration strategy. Photographs in the collection illustrate views from the Outlook Tower as well as interiors of the Tower's 'Edinburgh Room' showing the distribution of survey exhibits. Other photographs show the entrance of the Camera Obscura, with plants and greenery.

In its six floors, the building housed not only Geddes's architectural and planning offices but also an international and colourful variety of people from all walks of life when Geddes attracted and encouraged to stay. Among them were artists, poets, geographers, anarchists, philosophers, writers, who aimed by their interaction to inspire one another along the evolutionary upwards spiral towards The Ascent of Man.

The Tower (now lost to the public under its current management) was organised as an Index Museum and was rightly called a sociological laboratory, where the Geddes thinking was represented in three dimensions. With it, he aimed to change the attitudes of the next generation and it became an urban observatory where live issues of the city were viewed and discussed, and where people could learn how best to interact with their environment.

Meanwhile, at the other end of the Royal Mile, Geddes convinced Dr Barbour and his sister, also members of the Social Union, to buy Whitehorse Close in the Canongate. This historic courtyard building is the last survivor of its type in Edinburgh and was later renovated by the firm of Sir Frank Mears.

Geddes was fully acquainted with Ruskin's writings and aesthetically close to Capper's romanticism; this may have been why Capper was chosen to develop the Geddes *pièce de résistance*, the Ramsay Garden development – an architectural triumph. This was to be the new element to culminate the regeneration of the Old Town, which so far had included: conservation, rehabilitation, conservative demolition. Now, finally, new construction.

Geddes purchased the garden ground of the existing late 18th century villa of the poet Allan Ramsay, on the north slope of Castlehill. Having already attracted students to live in the Old Town, Geddes set

FIG 14
Outlook Tower Biological Room
(Patrick Geddes Archive, University of Edinburgh)

out to attract also lecturers of the University by providing: '...a rich and delightful living background – be one student or professor.'

The fashion at the time was for building in the neo-classical style, but Geddes wanted something vernacular in a national romantic style and with a great deal of historical references, yet with the most up to date lighting and services.

Typically, Geddes's brief to the architect was:

> ...take the house of the poet as an irritant in an oyster and build me a pearl around it.

Henbest Capper, in 1892, and Sydney Mitchell, in 1893, both rose to the challenge and they built for Geddes a pearl in the form of a five-storey block of flats deriving from, but transforming too, the traditional Scottish tenement form. Ramsay Garden, in a unique site commanding spectacular views over Edinburgh, the Forth and Fife, is one of the great buildings of Edinburgh and in setting and style totally fulfils its original brief.

The University Hall Extension, the part of the complex facing north, was formally opened in 1894 to occupation by students. Life in the halls must have been not only comfortable, but above all inspiring, with abundance of comfort and an artistic environment with spectacular views. This was the setting for Geddes's Edinburgh Summer Meetings, with their interdisciplinary curriculum and memorable evening parties.

The building was decidedly modern. It had an electricity supply and a telephone connection, one of the first in Edinburgh, its number in two digits only. The sanitary arrangements were the last word in design and convenience and there was even an ingenious form of ducted warm air central heating. The whole venture was financed by the methods used in the Old Town improvements, an early type of housing co-operative; each prospective owner-occupier bought their flat in advance of its construction, in a rolling fund. As Geddes would say:

> Housing is nothing unless it is the building of homes where men and women and children can really live.

The Photographs Now

The surviving photographic collection consists of approximately 240 glass-plate negatives (or slides), which were originally stored at the Outlook Tower and were used by Geddes to illustrate his survey of Edinburgh, as we have seen above. The total collection may well have been larger: some of the extremely fragile slides could have been broken in the material's many moves over the years.

In the case of glass negatives found in their original envelopes, the location of the scene depicted was indicated in handwriting on the envelope. The notes are in three different hands and, after examining the handwriting, with the help of Miss Elspeth Yeo of the National Library of Scotland, it was possible to establish that the hands are those of Alasdair Geddes, Patrick's eldest son; Robert Dykes, an Edinburgh photographer; and Mabel Barker, Geddes's goddaughter and assistant. A fourth assistant in the work of assembling the photographs for the original exhibition at the Outlook Tower and the subsequent Cities Exhibition at the Royal Academy in London was Norah Geddes. However, no evidence of her handwriting was found on the envelopes.

After a long time in storage with the rest of the Geddes material, sorting was begun in 1985 by myself and later completed by Miss E.C.I. Fortescue, at the Patrick Geddes Centre for Planning Studies. The centre had been created as part of the then Department of Urban Design and Regional Planning of the University of Edinburgh, and is now closed.

The bulk of the photographs depict views of the city, ranging from broad panoramas to close-up street scenes. These are arranged in the catalogue according to their districts outwards from the Outlook Tower, beginning with the Castle and the Tower itself. Other plates, such as of maps and diagrams, the Outlook Tower interior and a few under the heading 'Childhood and the Environment', are grouped at the end.

The photographs were not meant merely to provide visual entertainment for the people of Edinburgh or visitors to the city. In many cases they were meant to shock the authorities into action by showing, rather, the areas of decay and dereliction. They showed haphazard development of industrial sites, and wholesale demolition, as well as appalling housing and homelessness, aspects of the city that Geddes deplored. Abercrombie referred to the 'nightmare of the Edinburgh Room'.

FIG 15
Area Garden, St Andrew Square
(Patrick Geddes Archive, University of Edinburgh)

Where good practice was found, it was recorded and displayed *pour encourager les autres*. While it was not possible to find the exact location of FIG 15, PLATE 8B shows that the century since the survey has not been all progress. The photographs pointed out also where it was possible to provide a better environment for the local residents and for future generations. There are many pictures of children.

The Patrick Geddes Collection of Edinburgh Photographs is now at the Edinburgh University Library, together with the rest of the Archival Collection of the Geddes Papers. Slides have been identified. They are in new envelopes and special boxes. Volume II of the catalogue produced by the Patrick Geddes Centre, before its closure, is entirely dedicated to the Edinburgh Survey Photographs, and copies of the slides can be seen in the published catalogue. A visit to the University Library Geddes Collection will provide researchers with an insight into the problems Geddes was tackling in Edinburgh at the time, and a better understanding of the magnitude of the regeneration work he and his associates accomplished in their attempt to turn the trend of dereliction and degradation into one of hope for the future.

The glass plates are now safe and they constitute an excellent base-line for comparison with future surveys. However, it is important to secure further funding for a special conservation project for the Geddes photographs before they deteriorate any further.

Outside Edinburgh, the survey was first exhibited in October 1910 in London at the Royal Academy, on the invitation of Sir Patrick Abercrombie, as part of the famous Cities and Town Planning Exhibition organised by the Royal Institute of British Architects in the Galleries of the Royal Academy.

The impact of the survey was felt deeply by followers of Geddes. They are many; among others Patrick Abercrombie, George Pepler, Raymond Unwin and Ebenezer Howard in England; Lewis Mumford in America; Frank and Mary Tindall and Bob Grieve in Scotland; Percy Johnson-Marshall in Britain and in India. Further afield, they include, too, John Turner, Kenneth Watts, Max Lock, in South America, South East Asia and Africa respectively. Thus the seeds of the Geddesian Survey were spread far and wide.

In Geddes's own words:

Our Civic Survey, thus has ranged through wide limits, from the fullest civic idealism on the one hand, to the most direct and ruthless realism on the other. For there is no real incompatibility between the power of seeing things as they are... and the power of things as they may be... *(Transactions of the Cities and Town Planning Exhibition, Edinburgh 1911)*

Appendix
Edinburgh Social Union

(ANNE M. MATHAMS OF EDINBURGH is the daughter of the late Mrs Annie M. Mathams, who died in 1977. In the paper above, Sofia Leonard, in a 'top-down' account, has clarified the relationship between Geddes, the Edinburgh Social Union and the photographic survey. Miss Mathams's notes below look at the union from the standpoint of one engaged in its daily routine. As we know, Geddes was strong on development and weak on maintenance. Here we catch a little of the dedication and purpose of one whose duty it was to keep the system running effectively and humanely. We can observe something of the dedication of those in the organisation who were able to keep it going long after the initial Geddes impulse was exhausted and, indeed, for some 20 years and another world war after his death – Editor)

Edinburgh Social Union

My mother – Mrs Annie M. Mathams – was one of the first five women in Britain to be trained as HM Inspectors of Factories. After Glasgow University (where she was in the same class as her future husband) from 1907 she began work in Ireland, in manufacturing industry and fisheries. She continued in central Scotland, where she married. She then became a war widow, from the First Great War, with two young children. She was employed by the Edinburgh Social Union and appreciated the chance to undertake social service in the community. It came to an end about 1945 and she finally retired at the age of 65 years.

The aims of the Edinburgh Social Union were to provide the care and upkeep of various town properties and to maintain personal contact with the tenants, giving any help required. A team of about six or eight women was employed for this purpose and each house was visited each week. Where possible, rent and savings bank money were collected and problems such as repairs, arrears, complaints about bad behaviour etc. were dealt with. Typical rents were 4/5d (22p) for a 'single end' – a house of one room – and 6/8d (33p) for a 'double end' – two rooms.

The women were also involved with the change of tenancy in the houses and they interviewed new tenants, attending to any business involved.

As a small girl, I often accompanied my mother, and remember at first-hand her concerns – the need to care for the houses, cleaning rooms and furniture, the importance of the cleaning of chimneys, and fumigating the rooms because of bed bugs and the infectious diseases of the time, especially tuberculosis. In many cases a 'buggie van' was involved. Hot water depended on the kitchen range; overcrowding meant that there were not enough chairs to seat everyone and 'truckle beds' were common – these were small beds on castors kept under a bed or beds during the day. Repairs were assessed and negotiated – 'Auld wifie needs an auld wife' (Old lady requires a cowl for her smoking chimney).

Social support was the order of the day, and emphasis was placed on befriending the families in the houses and giving kindly help when it was needed during times of illness and when a death occurred in the home. My mother took food to the ill. To boost morale, bulbs were handed out and an annual flower show held. As was the occasional baby show. I remember tales of the desperate young couples being interviewed for a vacant house. Often one person would collect the rents for their neighbours on the common stair. I remember the time when a professional man's widow was found a single room at 20p on the top floor of an eight-storey historic tenement. Crippled by arthritis, all her shopping and necessities had to be fetched by others in the stair. But, in return, she looked after babies when their mothers had to go out. The slightly older ones she helped with their homework, and she could act as an honest broker in disputes. Also, there were moments of near-comedy, as when my mother was ordered, 'Will ye get doon on your knees, and look under the bed.' This was to find that she was being presented with a splendid majolica cheese dish. I was treated to a special performance when one old lady, who had been on the stage, lifted her skirts and sang and danced for me. When we were children, recovering from childhood illnesses, our mother would go out of her way to bring home a bag of 'recovery cakes' as she called them. They were fondant cream boat tarts from McVities in Princes Street and much enjoyed by us, and were general favourites.

None of the women employed with the Edinburgh Social Union had specific training or a social work degree for this work but all had a social conscience. In my mother's case, she was well qualified for work with people because of her experience as a factories inspector. This also gave her good organisational experience. I remember the Misses Marion and Beatrice Stewart, and Miss Salmon, a leading light in the Girl Guides, who dealt with office work. Each Thursday morning she collected rent and savings bank money in an office in Melville Street. What does it tell us about civic order in Edinburgh that, on the same day of every week for years, along the same routes through some of the worst housing in Western Europe, several unaccompanied women carried bags of cash without any untoward incident whatever? Yet many were quite desperate, to the extent that I remember a father regularly pawning the coat of his 'dear wee girl' to pay the rent on Monday, getting it out again with his wages on Friday so that she could wear it to church on Sunday.

As far as is known by me, my mother was involved in the following town properties:

Gladstone's Land	Castle Wynd
Riddle's Court	Milne's Court
Old Playhouse Close	
White Horse Close	
Bible Land and Shoemaker's Close	
Abbey Strand	
Some properties in Arthur Street	
East and Middle Arthur Place	
Waverley Buildings	
Blackfriars Street	
Drumdryan Street; and, I believe,	
Some parts of Leith.	

I have clear memories of accounts given to me by my mother from my childhood onwards and I paid visits to the homes of those she particularly befriended.

Cartoons by Hendrik Willem Van Loon: Geddes, Van Loon, and Mumford

Walter Stephen

THIS ESSAY LOOKS AT THREE interesting men whose ideas have been burned into our minds so that we often think of them as our own. Each was distinguished in his own field but in 1925 they interacted actively to some purpose. The central focus of this book is Patrick Geddes, and an examination of this interaction will add something to our understanding of this great man, by that date somewhat in decline. These men led busy, complex lives. Perhaps the best way to start is with a selective timeline.

Ages and Status of Principals

	Geddes	Van Loon	Mumford
1854	Born Ballater		
1882		Born Rotterdam	
1895			Born Flushing NY
1900, 1901	Visits to USA		
1905		Cornell University	
1910–1914	Cities Exhibition		
1913		*Fall of the Dutch Republic*	
1915	*Cities in Evolution*		Stimulated by PG
1914–15, 1915–17, 1919–23	Visits to India		
1917	Deaths of Anna and Alasdair		
1919	Retirement (Dundee)		
1920			Columbia University
1922			*The Story of Mankind Survey* founded in NY
1923	Third visit to USA		First meets PG
1924	Scots College set up		

| 1925 | Montpellier, Jerusalem, Montpellier, Cambridge, Edinburgh, Montpellier | 5 days at Outlook Tower |

From 1 February 1925 (Six) *Talks from My/The Outlook Tower, in Survey, cartoons by Hendrick Van Loon*

1929		First radio broadcast	
1930			Stanford University
1931	Only radio broadcast		
1932	Knighthood, Death	Regular broadcasts	
1933		*The Home of Mankind*	
1934			*Technics and Civilization*
1938		*The Arts of Mankind*	*Culture of Cities*
1939–40		Broadcasts to Holland	
1939–42		Work with Refugees	
1943		*Van Loon's Lives*	
1944		Died Old Greenwich CT	
1961			*The City in History*
1966			*Disciple's Rebellion*
1990			Died Dutchess County NY

1923, in which Geddes made an extended visit to the United States, was a crucial year. His wife, companion and bulwark of over 30 years had died in 1917, soon after the death of Alasdair, the elder and, it must be said, favourite son. In 1919 Geddes had had to retire from his Chair at Dundee. While never full-time, it had supplied him with a core income and a certain degree of structure in his intellectual life. The Chair of Sociology at Bombay certainly remedied some of that particular uncertainty, but commuting between continents was no way of ensuring the continuing success of his Edinburgh ventures.

For Geddes, 1923 started in Bombay. May to August was spent in the US, and the year ended in Bombay again. Lewis Mumford, who had long been an admirer of Geddes, met him off the boat, in the beginning of a relationship he described many years later in *The Disciple's Rebellion*. Geddes, now an old man, saw in Mumford the needed replacement for Alasdair. Geddes would be the developer and Mumford would provide the maintenance without which ideas and projects must founder. 1923 saw their first interaction face to face, and a summer of uneasy cooperation, while 1925 was to see Mumford's disillusion with the reality behind Geddes's persuasiveness.

Boardman sets the scene:

> The *Adriatic* docked in New York on 7 May, and the historic occasion was at hand for both imperious master and hesitant disciple. For close on five years they had exchanged ideas, made plans for collaboration in Palestine and India, and almost met in London in 1920.

Most of the summer was spent in New York, where Geddes gave a series of lectures on Geddesian City and Regional Planning at the New School for Social Research (where he had a room). Long before McLuhan, Geddes showed in these lectures the tension between the message and the medium. There was good sense for those who attended – 'young architects and the usual vague sprinkling of females' – but who could discern it? Geddes's delivery was poor. The idea of a series of articles was mooted by the *Survey Graphic*, a social workers' weekly, and a stenotypist was brought in. The result was 'a terrible botch'.

However, the core material was too good to lose and Geddes revised and rewrote until six articles were published monthly as 'Talks from My/The Outlook Tower' from February to September 1925. (The series started from 'My' Outlook Tower, and changed quickly to 'The' Outlook Tower).

From internal evidence, some of the work was done on board ship, a reminder for us that Geddes, who travelled a great deal, was as active on the move as the modern businessman with his laptop. ('As I revise this manuscript, our ship is running along the east coast of Sicily, between Messina and Catania' – there follows a description of the coastal detritus and malarial breeding grounds of the Mediterranean.)

The articles are fascinating and have been a main source for all writers on Geddes. Before analysing them, we must look at the third party in this collaboration.

Hendrik Willem Van Loon, of the three principals, is probably the least well known to British people today, but he was by no means a negligible figure. For this writer, he was the first of the three encountered. If one had to choose a book other than the Bible and the complete works of Shakespeare to take to a desert island, *Van Loon's Lives* would certainly be on the short list. First published in 1943 and set on the island of Walcheren, then under occupation by the Nazis, it is dedicated to Juliana (later Queen of the Netherlands) and:

> those valiant men of our beloved Zeeland who died while try-
> ing to preserve and maintain that most cherished of their pos-
> sessions their LIBERTY. (*Van Loon's capitals*)

Ostensibly an interesting collection of essays on important historical figures, sugared by being set, imaginatively, in the town of Veere, *Van Loon's Lives* is really a justification and a plea for liberal democracy in a world dominated by fascism.

Van Loon was born in Rotterdam in 1882, looked at the world through Dutch/European eyes, yet spent most of his life in the United States. As a child he loathed the sort of 'education' that was forced upon him, and at the age of 12 he had started and discontinued a Universal Historical Encyclopedia. From his later writings we can adduce that he found the Holland of his youth narrow and censorious, prejudiced and concerned with the niceties of religion rather than its central message. At 20 he went to America out of sheer curiosity, having begun to study English seriously only three years previously (after reading Thackeray's *Henry Esmond*). He graduated brilliantly in history at Cornell University (1905) and spent a year at Harvard, becoming a journalist and passing through the Russian Revolution of 1906–7. After five years' further study of history in Munich (PhD, 1911) he returned to America to teach in universities, but during the 1914–19 war he was again travelling all over Europe as a reporter.

In 1921 he launched upon the world *The Story of Mankind*, in which he tried to make history picturesque. The success of this revolutionary book was phenomenal; it was translated into 14 languages, and both its matter and its illustrations (all drawn by the author) aroused intense controversy. It gave the approach to history that enlightened parents and teachers had been needing. It made history live and earned Van Loon the Newberry Medal. Between the wars he continued his flow of substantial and stimulating contributions to popular under-standing, interspersed with pioneer radio broadcasts and lectures for the Cunard Line.

During the Second World War he broadcast to occupied Holland from Boston and worked on his varied humanitarian concerns – aiding refugees from Nazi persecution and war-relief fund raising. He died in Old Greenwich, Connecticut in 1944. He did not live to see the liberation of Walcheren in November 1944.

His main achievement was the steady flow of major popular texts, ostensibly aimed at children. The style is easy and conversational, but the palette is global and the approach thematic. The big issues are never ducked. It is illuminating to read that Van Loon wrote for children, in the year of my birth:

> We are all fellow-passengers on the same planet, and we are all equally responsible for the happiness and well-being of the world in which we happen to live.

In the Rembrandthuis in the Jodenbreestraat of Amsterdam are no great biblical scenes, no great portraits in oils. Instead there is an intimate collection of Rembrandt's lesser works, pencil drawings and little sketches using pen and ink. Often no more than a few ink scrawls on a piece of white paper, the white seems to have three dimensions and the result is a miracle of expression. Van Loon obviously took Rembrandt as a model when he illustrated his own books.

Van Loon's drawings are more than illustrations inserted to break up the text. At first one may wonder why a respectable publisher bothered to use them; then their significance begins to grow. Van Loon drew excellent sketch maps to clear up a point. Like Geddes, they often register because of a change of perspective, or imaginative reconstruction. Today they look interesting, quirky, even amateurish; but in their time they were mind-stretching.

In Veere, Van Loon's name is not forgotten – indeed, in the fish shop they were able to tell me at once which house he had lived in and where the plaque was. But he is remembered for the oddest achievement – yet it is quite Geddesian. In the 1920s, he started regattas in the harbour of Veere for the traditional fishing boats of Walcheren, already threatened by the forces of homogenisation and globalisation. How like Geddes – Maharajah for the Day at Indore! Local participation and public spectacle as a force for community building. But how unlike Geddes in that Van Leer's institution has survived into the 21st century!

Geddes had a high opinion of Van Loon. In the *Talks from the Outlook Tower* he says:

We are thus brought face to face with the enormous and laborious studies of histories, literatures, origins, to which Van Loon or Wells give excellent introductory primers

and again:

Wells' *Outline [The Outline of History,* 1920*]* seems to be having a widely educative result, on both sides of the Atlantic, in abating too nationalistic sympathies; as also Van Loon's and, of course, more specialised works.

It is likely that Geddes and Van Loon met in 1923 and a decision was made that the *Talks* should be illustrated by 'cartoons' drawn by Van Loon – cartoons in the original sense of 'a full-size preparatory sketch for a fresco, tapestry, mosaic etc...' as in Leonardo da Vinci. It might be considered that Van Loon was being patronised when he was chosen as a mere illustrator, given his pedigree, but we must give Geddes and Mumford credit for recognising that Van Loon was a 'name' who would add credibility to the *Talks* when published and whose perceptions would add to Geddes's text.

There is a temptation to report at length on the *Talks*. What follows is the barest minimum consistent with the effective teasing out of parallels and implications.

The first *Talk* ('A Schoolboy's Bag and A City's Pageant') was published on 1 February 1925, in volume 53 of *Survey*, with a Foreword by Lewis Mumford, entitled: 'Who is Patrick Geddes?' In my introduction we saw how he found Geddes to be 'a vigorous institution'. He went on to say that:

...his work and his philosophy have sprung out of the fullness of his life, as Hermes the traveller, as Apollo the thinker, as Ares the husband and father, as Hercules the cleanser of the slums of Edinburgh, and now, at the summit of his life, as Jove, the wise parent of spirit-children scattered about the world in

New York, Bombay, Calcutta, Indore, Jerusalem, Edinburgh, Montpelier, London, and where not.

A living legacy, indeed!

His conclusion is a challenge to his readers:

And as the Tower embodies a new outlook, a new method, a fresh mode of life, wherever that vision is seen, and that mode followed, some new avatar of the Tower must arise. 'Why not,' as Professor Geddes would quickly urge, 'in America?'

We have seen how the cover of *Dramatisations of History* showed a naked god-like Geddes reclining over the paws of a sphinx. The first part of the first *Talk* starts off with the Schoolboy's Bag and other recycled elements from *Dramatisations*. (There is an echo of Dewey's Education of Head, Heart and Hand here. When he had three children to educate, Geddes visited 'Professor Dewey's early experimental school at Chicago', in 1899 and 1900. It was 'found of real encouragement and stimulus.' Each man greatly impressed the other.)

Geddes is honestly self-critical in his uncertainty about how to achieve civic development. For the Outlook Tower: 'the result after a generation is still but small'. Crosby Hall was 'a success d'estime' but had 'no popular interest'. 'Le Play House... has still a struggle'. Only once, he said, 'have we really laid hold of the imagination of a whole community', at Indore, where, as Maharajah for a day, he led a public health campaign. Uncharacteristically for Geddes, he gives us a statistic. When the average life expectancy in Britain was 50, and in India 30, Indore was India's most disease-ridden city, with a life expectancy of 18.6 years.

Positively, he records that 700 out of 1,000 flats have been taken up in a planned garden suburb, and ends by pointing out the relevance of his message to American cities. They need stir and festivals to awaken them from their daily routine; and from the depression, even stagnation, of civic thought and hope. A final touch is to show how much can be done with so little, by a single piper (Alasdair) leading the children 'to some new Children's Garden, henceforth their own for work and play.'

'Cities and the Soils They Grow From' is the first lecture in which Van Loon's cartoons appear. Geddes starts with a mention of the Outlook Tower and the (implied) resemblance of it to: 'the high office building which (financially speaking) your Mr Wrigley built out of chewing gum.' The theme is the city in 'the matrix of a vastly and minutely complex and heterogenous world.' We start from 'the elementary division of human labor':

FIG 16
The elementary division
of human labor
('Talks from My/
The Outlook Tower')

and pass on to show the interaction around the Mediterranean of deforestation, its effect on rainfall and drainage:

FIG 17
When the trees are
gone...
('Talks from My/
The Outlook Tower')

Part of the decline of much of the whole Mediterranean followed the growth of malaria and the decline of cultivation, plus the devastation of productive forests by war.

FIG 18
The city could not but decline
('Talks from My/
The Outlook Tower')

But Geddes is not despondent; he extols the virtues of arboriculture and gives late-19th century examples of how ruined landscapes can be turned around.

With 'The Valley Plan of Civilization' we are on familiar territory, as the Valley Section must be Geddes's best-known model, or 'thinking machine'. 'Broadly speaking, this way the world is built,' says Geddes, and there is still mileage to be obtained from the application of his model to the world of today. Individualisation of transport, the transmissibility of power, flexibility of labour, all seem to have destroyed the almost deterministic relationships Geddes saw between nature and man's occupations – and yet knowledge and understanding can still result from a consideration of the Valley Section.

He starts with some thoughts about war. 'Wars are not fundamental to human history'. 'Essential to have as clear an understanding as we may of normal life-processes before we come to pathological interruptions.' 'So before coming (or going) to War, let us learn more of the ways of Peace.' He contrasts wheat- and rice-growing communities and the tools for study – the atlas and the Great Globe of Reclus – before launching into a lengthy analysis of the Valley Section.

Van Loon's contribution is to provide for each environment/occupation a tiny cartouche, to set the scene, as it were.

FIG 19A
Forest Lands
(*'Talks from My/The Outlook Tower'*)

FIG 19B
Hill Pastures
(*'Talks from My/The Outlook Tower'*)

Geddes in this lecture plunges from close reasoning to wild generalisation. The reader may be forgiven for supposing that Charlie the goose is to be seen waddling back on to the village green. PG offers, for example, no evidence when considering the Sea Coast, for the 'strengthened individuality and self-reliance [of women] in those parts'. Surely he is straining too hard to make connections when he says:

> It is thus by no mere accident, but also from deep-rooted tradition that my old and honoured friend, the veteran president of the International Council of Women should bear the title of Marchioness of (the old fishing port of) Aberdeen.

The third *Talk* concludes with a rather neat realisation of the Valley Section in the Town, which becomes the subject of the next talk. In a typically Geddesian aphorism he states that: 'If we would be city-builders, we must first of all be archaeologist-historians', a reincarnation of his three doves – Survey, Synthesis, Synergy.

'The Education of Two Boys' is probably the talk of most interest to us today and has provided a rich resource for biographers. We might suppose the two boys would be Alasdair and Arthur, but they are, in fact, Alasdair and Geddes himself. Alasdair was the steady, capable lad who had a good war record but was killed in 1917. Arthur was the least able of the Geddes children to survive their uneven childhood – 'a brilliant and promising child – with nerves'.

Geddes pitches right in – 'Let me begin with mis-education' – with an attack on gambling and discussion of whether it should be repressed by law or checked by bettered education and conditions. The present system comes in for violent attack:

> Consider this biological view of such parents – who by abandoning their young to supposed (or even really gifted) super-parents provided with artificial orphanages called boarding-schools (or more accurately, standardising shops) – lapse necessarily, and to a serious extent, from the mammalian level, and its intelligence accordingly, since thus acquired in nature and needing to be developed in civilisation.

Yet Alasdair had decided he needed a year at Edinburgh Academy to make sure he was not disadvantaged by his lack of conventional schooling. Working on farms and at Millport Research Station, and an Arctic expedition, were not enough.

Geddes then proceeds to his own childhood and upbringing. His home and early adventures there and in the neighbouring Sidlaws are described: 'Kinnoull is a nobly wooded hill, with ... a long range of noble precipice'.

FIG 20

... a long range of noble precipice
('Talks from My/The Outlook Tower')

'Why here these reminiscences?' he asks us. 'Not merely from senescence and its reviving memory', but as an illustration of the Freudian view of the fundamental significance of early experience and impressions upon later life. He recognises that all children could not be as fortunate as he had been, but points out the importance of the Boy Scouts and Girl Guides in providing experiences outside the home. In his case, a tendency to mischief was cured by 'the wise father' who had an outdoor lean-to shed erected as laboratory; and with carpenter's bench as well.

FIG 21
In this case our conversion was to the new and frightful joys of experimental chemistry
('Talks from My/The Outlook Tower')

The last talk was published in September 1925, although it had been written well before then. In that month Geddes was living in the Outlook Tower, trying 'to tidy up the middens of notes and manuscripts'. Mumford, lecturing in Geneva, was invited by Geddes to visit him. Mumford's first visit to Edinburgh lasted five days. He camped in the library, amid bookcases and boxes of notes. His adolescent dream had come true: 'but with the fingermarks of reality, as usual, smudging the shining surface.'

The visit was not a success. Mumford felt he was neglected by his host. Geddes appealed for help with the Sisyphean task of tidying his papers. On the top floor of the Outlook Tower, after using the Camera Obscura, Geddes insisted in forcing on Mumford his interpretation of the landscape, even taking him by the shoulders to ensure he was seeing what Geddes was seeing and giving the correct response. 'That settled it,' wrote Mumford. 'Much as I admired Geddes, much though I valued his help, I would not see Edinburgh or aught else through his eyes. If any single moment marked the ultimate parting of our ways, this was the moment, and that rooftop the place.' It was of this experience that Mumford graphically said: 'Tidying up after Geddes was like trying to put the contents of Vesuvius back into the crater after an eruption.'

After this incident, the lives of Geddes and Mumford diverged. The Scots College in some ways filled the vacuum in PG's life. Mumford went his own distinguished but more conventional way. Not till 1966, in *The Disciple's Rebellion*, was he able properly to sort out the complexity of the relationship, and apportion blame without rancour. As for Van Loon, the timeline shows that his relationship with Geddes and Mumford had been tangential and he was able to continue in his useful and entertaining way, writing big popular books and reaching a wide public through the media of his time – something that Geddes was never able to do.

A Geddes Chronology

1854	Born 2 October, in Ballater, youngest of five children
1857	Family moved to Mount Tabor, Perth
1871	Left Perth Academy for work in bank and 'free home studies'
1874	Biology at Edinburgh (one week) and London (under Huxley)
1878	Roscoff (Brittany) and the Sorbonne
1879	Set up Scottish Zoological Station at Cowie, Stonehaven
	The Mexican Adventure
1880	Demonstrator in Botany, Edinburgh University
1882	Letter from Charles Darwin (quoted by Aubrey Manning)
1886	Marriage to Anna Morton
1887	Norah Geddes born
	University Hall, first self-governing hostel
1887–1900	Summer schools set up and run every August
1888	Professor of Botany, University College, Dundee
1891	Alasdair Geddes born
1892	Outlook Tower started
1893	Ramsay Garden created as co-operative flats
1895	Arthur Geddes born
1897	Cyprus – survey and planning
1900	Held International Assembly at *Exposition Universelle*, Paris
	First visit to United States
	Return visit to United States
1903	Dunfermline development plan and publication of *City Development*

1908	Crosby Hall (Chelsea) relocated and restored as residence for university women
1910	Cities Exhibition at Chelsea (then toured till lost at sea 1914)
1913	Cities Exhibition awarded Grand Prix in Ghent
1914–15	First visit to India (with Alasdair)
1915	*Cities in Evolution* published
1915–17	Second visit to India (with Anna)
1917	Deaths of Alasdair and Anna
1919	Retirement and Farewell Lecture (Dundee)
	Planning in Jerusalem and Tel Aviv
	Professor of Civics and Sociology at Bombay
1919–23	Third visit to India (with Arthur)
1923	Third visit to USA
1924	Left Bombay for Montpellier (health reasons)
	Collège des Écossais founded
1925	Civil List pension of £80 awarded
1926	Compensation of £2,000 paid for loss of Cities Exhibition
	Geddes's plan for city of Tel Aviv accepted
1928	Marriage to Lilian Brown
1932	Offer of knighthood accepted – accolade 25 February
	Death at Montpellier – 17 April
1956	Frank Fraser Darling published *Pelican in the Wilderness: A Naturalist's Odyssey in North America*
1962	*Silent Spring* – Rachel Carson
1969	Reith Lectures – *Wilderness and Plenty* (Frank Fraser Darling)
1972	*Blueprint for Survival* (*The Economist*)
1973	Establishment of Sir Patrick Geddes Memorial Trust

	'Geddes-awareness' campaign started by *Bulletin of Environmental Education*
1974	*Small is Beautiful: Economics as if People Mattered* – E.F. Schumacher
1975	*A Most Unsettling Person* – Paddy Kitchen
1978	*The Worlds of Patrick Geddes* – Patrick Boardman
1982	Commemorative events in several locations, home and abroad
1985	Patrick Geddes Centre for Planning Studies set up (in the Outlook Tower)
1990	*Patrick Geddes: Social Evolutionist and City Planner* – Helen Meller
1991–92	International Summer Meetings run by Patrick Geddes Centre
1992	Rio Earth Summit and Local Agenda 21
2004	Geddes Garden at Scots College, Montpellier, restored
	Ideas in Evolution – Geddes 150th Anniversary Symposium, Edinburgh
	Patrick Geddes: The Regeneration of Edinburgh – Anniversary Exhibition at the Matthew Gallery, University of Edinburgh
	Think Global, Act Local: The Life and Legacy of Patrick Geddes – Walter Stephen (ed)

Select Bibliography

Detailed references and bibliographies for each contribution would have interfered with the readability of the text, as well as being unnecessarily repetitive. The following nine sources can be regarded as the 'basic kit' and have been used, to a greater or lesser extent, by all the contributors.

Philip Boardman, The *Worlds of Patrick Geddes* (Routledge and Kegan Paul, 1978)

Amelia Defries, *The Interpreter Geddes: The Man and His Gospel* (Routledge, London, 1927)

Gifford, MacWilliam and Walker, *The Buildings of Scotland: Edinburgh* (Penguin Books Ltd, 1984)

Paddy Kitchen, *A Most Unsettling Person* (Victor Gollancz, London, 1975)

Sofia Leonard, *The Regeneration of the Old Town of Edinburgh by Patrick Geddes* (*Planning History* Vol 21 No 2, February 1999)

Murdo Macdonald (ed), *Patrick Geddes: Ecologist, Educator, Visual Thinker* (*Edinburgh Review*, Issue 88, Summer 1992)

Philip Mairet, *The Life and Letters of Patrick Geddes* (Lund Humphries, London, 1957)

Helen Meller, *Patrick Geddes, Social Evolutionist and City Planner* (Routledge, 1990)

Walter Stephen (ed), *Think Global, Act Local: The Life and Legacy of Patrick Geddes* (Luath Press, Edinburgh, 2004)

A full Geddes bibliography can be found on the Sir Patrick Geddes Memorial Trust website (www.patrickgeddestrust.co.uk/new_site)

Important references to the individual contributions are given below, by contribution.

Introduction

Patrick Geddes, *Dramatisations of History* (Sociological Publications Ltd, London; Patrick Geddes and Colleagues, Edinburgh, 1923)

Michael Storm, Schools and the Community: An Issue-Based Approach (*Bulletin of Environmental Education*, May 1971)

Overkill

The Bible, Psalm 24 v 1; Matthew Ch 6 v 33, Ch 19 v22–26, Ch 25 v 35–36; Acts Ch 2 v 44–45

Brandt Commission Report, North–South: A Programme for Survival (Pan Books, 1980)

Christian Aid News (Summer, 2000)

Chronicle of the Second World War (Longman, 1990)

'Development Aid by 22 Countries, 1997–98' (OECD Statistics)

Al Gore, *Earth in the Balance* (Earth Scan, 1992)

Richard Lamb, *War in Italy, 1943–45: A Brutal Story* (John Murray, 1993)

Andrew Phillips, *The Love of Money* (The Hibbert Trust, 1988)

R.J. Sider, *Rich Christians in an Age of Hunger* (Hodder and Stoughton, 1978)

Frederick Turner, *John Muir: From Scotland to the Sierra* (Canongate, 1997)

Dunbar to Berwick: A Special Part of the East Coast Main Line

Angus Graham, 'Archaeology on a Great Post Road' (*Proceedings of the Society of Antiquaries of Scotland*, vol XCVI, 1962–63)

'East Coast Main Line: Dunbar to Berwick and Gradient Profile' – specially drawn by Norman Thomson.

Where was Peter Geddes born?

The Geddes Family Letters 1829–1865: with a supplement from Mount Tabor 1860–1888

Robert J. Naismith, *Buildings of the Scottish Countryside* (Gollancz, London, 1985)

Diana M. Henderson, *Highland Soldier: 1820–1920* (John Donald, Edinburgh, 1989)

Joanna Richardson, *Victoria and Albert* (Dent, London, 1977)

Miss Geddes's Dresden Establishment

Patrick Durnin, *Tillies: Tillie and Henderson Shirt Factory* (Guildhall Press, Derry, 2005)

Upton Sinclair, *World's End* (T Werner Laurie Ltd, London, 1940)

Frederick Taylor, *Dresden: Tuesday 13 February 1945* (Bloomsbury, London 2004)

Robert M. Young, *Belfast and the Province of Ulster in the 20th Century* (W.T. Burke and Co, Brighton, 1909)

Archive Sources:

Saxon State and Universities Library

Dresden City Archive

Saxon Academy of Science

Dresden Directory

Dresden City Library

Dresden Historical Society

Dresden High School of Music

Dr Ullrich Amlung, Dresden school history researcher

Alison Cairns, foreign correspondent

Through A Glass, Clearly

Roy Pinkerton and William J. Windram, *Three Hundred Years of Lawnmarket Heritage* (University of Edinburgh, 1983)

Cartoons by Hendrik Willem Van Loon

Patrick Geddes, *Dramatisations of History* (Sociological
Publications Ltd, London; Patrick Geddes and Colleagues,
Edinburgh, 1923)

Hendrik Willem Van Loon, *Van Loon's Lives* (Harrap, London,
1943)

Hendrik Willem Van Loon, *The Home of Mankind* (Harrap,
London, 1933 reprint)

Think Global, Act Local: The Life and Legacy of Patrick Geddes
Edited by Walter Stephen
ISBN 1 84282 079 6 PBK £12.99

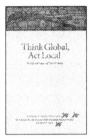

Town planning. Interest-led, open-minded education. Preservation of buildings with historical worth. Community gardens. All are so central to modern society that our age tends to claim these notions as its own. In fact they were first visualised by Sir Patrick Geddes, a largely forgotten Victorian Scot and one of the greatest forward thinkers in history.

Think global, act local
Patrick Geddes, Cities in Evolution, 1915

Vivendo discimus – by living we learn
By leaves we live

Gardener, biologist, conservationist, social evolutionist, peace warrior, and town planner, Geddes spent many years conserving and restoring Edinburgh's historic Royal Mile at a time when most decaying buildings were simply torn down. With renovation came educational ideas such as the development of the Outlook Tower, numerous summer schools and his Collège des Écossais in Montpellier. In India much of Geddes's belief in people planning can be seen, taking the form of pedestrian zones, student accommodation for women, and urban diversification projects.

Think Global, Act Local examines the life of this important man, who in recent years has become almost a patron saint of the sustainable development movement, and the continuing relevance of his ideas and their place in our world, present and future.

★★★★ *Super – Arguably the most important Scottish thinker of the 20th century... The contributors to this exciting new collection argue that Geddes's time has finally come.*

THE SCOTSMAN

Should be studied in Scottish secondary schools and the Scottish Parliament.

SCOTS MAGAZINE

An exploration and explication of the interdependence of the two strands of activity, environmental and cultural. Breathless catalogues, but they are fascinating.

PROSPECT

Willie Park Junior: The Man Who Took Golf to the World

Walter Stephen

ISBN 1 905222 21 1 HBK £25.00

 In the 19th century, Musselburgh, Scotland was a hotbed of golfing genius. The local links produced five Open Champions, and of these golfing greats, Willie Park Junior was undoubtedly more than just a good golfer. Park redefined the image of the golf professional and took the game from being an esoteric pastime, practised in a few favoured localities, to its present status as a worldwide game.

A two-time winner of the Open, Park also played challenge and demonstration matches at home and abroad. Ever the entrepreneur, his workshops turned out golf balls and clubs to his own design, with retail outlets in Edinburgh, Manchester, London, New York and Montreal, and Park was the first golf professional to write a manual – *The Game of Golf* – which appeared in 1896. His career in golf course design took him from Britain to Western Europe and then North America; in total Park lay out over 160 courses worldwide, over 40 of these in the United States and more than 20 in Canada, many of which are still in use today.

After a century of improved golf technology – better clubs, a larger ball, and more tailored course layouts – what legacy has Willie Park Junior left to the modern golfer? Walter Stephen tours us round some of Park's best-loved courses to see how they have stood the tests of time and tee-off.

Love and Revolution

Alastair McIntosh

ISBN 1 905222 58 0 PBK £8.99

 In *Soil and Soul: People Versus Corporate Power* Alastair McIntosh told of confronting the powers that be to transform a broken world. In this inspirational collection of poetry, he explores the nature of the revolutionary love that can bring healing. Here is poetry as a living force – a resource that can empower us all. From land ownership on the Isle of Eigg to saving the curlew, from the quiet solitude of a winter's night to passionate love, and loss beneath the ocean waves, Alastair McIntosh's poetry touches on and affirms all aspects of life's journey.

McIntosh's writing has been acclaimed by the feminist writer Starhawk as 'wonderful and inspiring', by Bishop James Jones of Liverpool as 'life-changing' and by Thom Yorke of Radiohead as 'truly mental'.

The book includes 'Homage to Young Men' as recorded with the chart-topping duo Nizlopi.

Emotional and thought provoking poems... his poetry very much reflects the Isles.

STORNOWAY GAZETTE

The Story of Loch Ness

Katharine Stewart

ISBN 1 84282 083 4 HBK £16.99

Known throughout the world for its legendary inhabitant, Loch Ness has inspired folklore and fascination in the hearts of those who visit it for centuries. But what of the characters, the history and the myths which enchanted inhabitants and travellers alike long before the first sightings of the so-called Loch Ness Monster? Katharine Stewart takes us on a journey through the past and the politics, the heroes and villains, and the natural beauties that are the true source of the magic of Loch Ness.

Where did the name Loch Ness come from, and how did Cherry Island come to be?

What can be said of the wildlife that makes its home around the loch?

Who determined the fate of the Loch Ness valley as we know it today?

While the depths and secrets of Loch Ness may never be revealed entirely, Stewart provides the answers to these and so many other questions in this compelling guide to one of Scotland's most famous places.

From geological origins to connections with the industrial revolution and speculation on the future of this national treasure, she presents a rich tapestry of unforgettable anecdotes.
SCOTLAND IN TRUST

At last – a book about Loch Ness without any of the usual 'Nessie' cliches and one written by a local author with a deep knowledge of the loch and its surroundings.
SCOTS MAGAZINE

It is invaluable as it is a statement in time and an important source of information about the loch.
HIGHLAND NEWS

Scotland – Land and People: An Inhabited Solitude

James McCarthy

ISBN 0 946487 57 X PBK £7.99

The new Scottish parliament is responsible for the environment of Scotland with the opportunity for land reform and new approaches to the protection and management of an incomparable countryside to meet the needs of the 21st century. It is difficult to avoid the conclusion that a far more radical approach is now required to safeguard the public interest over a very large proportion of Scotland's mountain and moorland country. There is little point in exhorting the unemployed, trapped in sub-standard inner city homes, to support campaigns for sustainable forestry or the protection of the Green Belt from industrial encroachment. The plain fact of the matter is that in Scotland, as elsewhere, the means of subsistence will always be first priority where this is under threat, and so-called environmentalists have too often been guilty of adopting an indifference to this.

Luath Press Limited

committed to publishing well written books worth reading

LUATH PRESS takes its name from Robert Burns, whose little collie Luath (*Gael.,* swift or nimble) tripped up Jean Armour at a wedding and gave him the chance to speak to the woman who was to be his wife and the abiding love of his life. Burns called one of 'The Twa Dogs' Luath after Cuchullin's hunting dog in *Ossian's Fingal.* Luath Press was established in 1981 in the heart of Burns country, and is now based a few steps up the road from Burns' first lodgings on Edinburgh's Royal Mile.

Luath offers you distinctive writing with a hint of unexpected pleasures.

Most bookshops in the UK, the US, Canada, Australia, New Zealand and parts of Europe either carry our books in stock or can order them for you. To order direct from us, please send a £sterling cheque, postal order, international money order or your credit card details (number, address of cardholder and expiry date) to us at the address below. Please add post and packing as follows: UK – £1.00 per delivery address; overseas surface mail – £2.50 per delivery address; overseas airmail – £3.50 for the first book to each delivery address, plus £1.00 for each additional book by airmail to the same address. If your order is a gift, we will happily enclose your card or message at no extra charge.

Luath Press Limited
543/2 Castlehill
The Royal Mile
Edinburgh EH1 2ND
Scotland
Telephone: 0131 225 4326 (24 hours)
Fax: 0131 225 4324
email: sales@luath.co.uk
Website: www.luath.co.uk